The
Hidden Man

The New Self

An Unveiling of the
Subconscious Mind

by

E. W. Kenyon

(edited and compiled

by

Ruth A. Kenyon)

Seventh Edition

Printed in U.S.A.

Copyright 1970

by

Kenyon's Gospel Publishing Society, Inc.

LYNNWOOD, WASHINGTON

E. W. KENYON

Author

TABLE OF CONTENTS

First Words

This is an unveiling of the "Hidden Man of the heart."

It is a study in what psychologists have called the "subconscious mind."

It is an attempt to reveal "yourself" to you.

Modern psychologists do not really know man, because man is a spirit, and they delve only in the realm of the Senses, thus they cannot become acquainted with the real man.

Man was created in the same class with God. He is an eternal spirit.

His senses were given to him to contact the physical world. He was given reasoning faculties so that he might use the knowledge that his senses conveyed to his brain.

Behind the sense-ruled reasoning faculties is the real man, who is a spirit.

The Church, as a whole, is unfamiliar with the recreated spirit.

What we call our conscience, is really the voice of the spirit. If one could learn to listen to his recreated spirit, and keep in intimate fellowship with the Father, there is no limit to where he could go in spiritual things.

The Holy Spirit was given to guide us into all truth, or reality. He finds it a very difficult thing to lead our reasoning faculties, but it is the normal and natural thing for Him to lead our spirits.

We have never realized that love is a product of the spirit, and not of the reasoning faculties. Faith is also a product of the spirit.

We are talking of the Recreated spirit which has received the nature and life of the Father. It has become united with Christ and received Eternal Life.

Eternal Life is the nature of the Father, and that nature is Love. Love is the mother of faith.

You can have no deep faith life without a love life.

The Recreated spirit is also the fountain of wisdom, and all of the other fruits of the spirit mentioned in Galatians 5:22.

I want you to study this book carefully, look up all of the references, and put the challenge to a real test.

5

Chapter The First

THE HIDDEN MAN OF THE HEART

OMETIME ago I was asked to write an article on the Psychology of the New Birth.

As I began to study the problem, I saw that there is no Psychology of the New Birth, for the New Birth is not mental, but spiritual.

Psychology has to do with the mind, and the New Birth has to do with the "hidden man of the heart," or the spirit of man.

You understand that man is in God's class of being. When he was created in the Garden he was made in the image and likeness of God. He had to be a spirit being because God is a Spirit.

He was created so that, by partaking of God's nature, he might become a child of God. If he were but a physical being he could not receive God's nature. If he were but a mental being, he could not receive God's nature.

He had to be a spirit being, an eternal being who would live as long as God lives. Man had to be in God's class.

He had to be created so that he could be the companion and associate of Deity.

God gave him authority over all the laws of nature. Every living thing was subject to him.

This same authority was evidently given to Jesus. During His earth walk He ruled the laws of nature, changed water into wine, restored the maimed limbs, calmed the seas, and raised the dead.

This first man was a spirit in God's class. When he committed High Treason he became a partaker of Satan's nature. He was actually born again, and he became a new Satanic creation. Because man is a spirit being, it was his spirit that partook of Satan's nature.

Before the fall in the Garden, during his fellowship with God, his spirit ruled him, and his senses were subject to his spirit. But, when he sinned, and his spirit received the nature of the Adversary, it became subordinated to his senses.

7

I believe that before Adam fell his five senses played only a small part; the instant he fell his spirit lost dominion, and his five senses took over. He now relied upon his senses: seeing, hearing, tasting, smelling and feeling.

He was driven from the presence of God. He was in an enemy world. He had to see clearly, lest he lose his life. He had to hear keenly, or an animal would take advantage of him. His taste must tell him what was good to eat. His touch must tell him whether an object was hot or cold, sharp, or rough.

Adam gained an education through his five senses.

His spirit was being made the prisoner of his five senses.

The Psalmist cried, "Bring my soul out of prison." Psalms 142:7.

The Hebrew word should have been translated "spirit" instead of "soul."

It was the cry of the spirit for liberty. It has been the cry for freedom down through the ages.

Man's spirit lost contact with God. His body became mortal, subject to death. This was the condition in which Jesus found the human race when He broke into the sense realm to introduce the Father to sense knowledge man.

Here are some spirit facts: man is a spirit, he has a soul. The soul is composed of his reasoning faculties. He lives in a physical body. The physical body possesses the five senses, they are the educators and teachers of the brain.

Let it be clearly understood that the brain cannot function without the senses.

If a child were born without sight, hearing, or feeling, he would be called an imbecile.

He may have just as good an intellect as the other children, but the senses have no way to contact it. The brain is dependent upon the five senses.

The spiritually dead man's spirit is in harmony with Satan. His spirit does not object if he commits murder.

You remember how Paul told Agrippa, "I lived in all good conscience." That was during the time he was consenting to the death of the believers.

His conscience permitted him to do it. That conscience was the voice of a spiritually dead man, a Satan-ruled spirit.

Here are some names that the spirit is called in the Epistles: the "Old Man" . . . "Put off the old man with its doings"; the "New Man" . . . "And put on the new man created after the image and likeness of God."

He is also called "the hidden man of the heart."

The spirit is the real man. The body is not the real man, it is merely the home in which the spirit lives.

The mind is not the real man, because the mind can be destroyed by destroying the senses.

The real man is the "hidden man of the heart," or the "hidden spirit."

Here is the proof of it: "Wherefore if any man is in Christ there is a new creation, the old things have passed away, behold they have become new. But all these things are of God."

He is called a New Creation.

Another translator makes it read like this: "Wherefore if any man is in Christ there is a new self."

That is in perfect harmony with Ez. 36:26 where the prophecy of a New Creation is given, "A new heart also will I give you, and a new spirit will I put within you."

The words "heart" and "spirit" are used interchangeably all through the Old and New Testaments.

God says that He is going to give man a new spirit. He is going to make a new man out of him. He is going to give him a new heart (or spirit) which will make him a New Creation.

What striking statements these are! Man is going to be Recreated. The sin nature is to be taken out of him. He will no longer be called the "Old Man." He is going to be called the "New Man" in Christ.

As the sinner, he is the "Old Man" who cannot approach God except through Christ; he does not know Him as a Father.

Now God has performed a miracle. He has recreated him. The "Old Man" has stopped being, and a "New Man" has taken his place. A New Creation comes into being.

This "hidden man of the heart" is now a "New Man," a new self.

The old self was born of spiritual death, the nature of the Adversary. The new self is born of love, the nature of the Father God.

He is a new Creation and he is created in Christ Jesus. He is going to have a new kind of walk.

The old self was in fellowship with the Adversary, the New Creation is in fellowship with the Father.

Here are a few valuable facts: the old creation had no standing with God. They could not approach Him. From the fall of man until Christ came, no human being could approach God except under the atoning blood of bulls and goats.

The New Creation man, who came into being on the Day of Pentecost, could stand in the Father's presence as though sin had never been.

"There is therefore now no condemnation to those who are in Christ Jesus."

"Who can lay anything to the charge of God's elect? It is God who has declared him righteous."

This New Creation man has become the righteousness of God in Christ.

You can now see that Christianity is God dealing with the spirit of man. He imparts to man His nature, making man a New Creation.

He is as much a New Creation as was Adam in the Garden.

God makes His contact with man through his spirit, not his senses.

The development of the human spirit is imperative.

We have wondered how this unseen, unknown personality could be developed. We know now.

He is a partaker of the Divine Nature.

The first manifestation of that Divine Nature is the new kind of love.

The development, then, of this New Creation is going to be by the nature of the Father taking him over.

In other words, he begins to walk in love, live the love life, practice the Word, and fellowship with the Father.

Jesus' earth walk was a perfect example of this new love life.

The Father can unveil the Word to a man's spirit so that it becomes a living thing in his daily walk.

Love becomes his natural realm. He lives love. He thinks love. He is love, because he is a child of love. God is love.

Chapter The Second

THE NEW SELF

AN is a spirit being. He possesses a physical body in which he dwells. He has a soul composed of his reasoning faculties. His body enables him to contact physical things. His reasoning faculties contact mental things. His spirit contacts spiritual things.

Before he receives Eternal life his spirit is dominated by Spiritual Death. This makes it impossible for him to understand the Bible, which is Revelation Truth.

I Cor. 2:14 "Now the natural man receiveth not the things of the spirit of God for they are foolishness unto him; and he cannot know them because they are spiritually understood."

The part of man that is recreated is his spirit.

Ezek. 11:19 is a remarkable prophecy. "And I will give them one heart, and I will put a new spirit within you: and I will take the stony heart out of their flesh and give them a heart of flesh."

Here is a unique suggestion. He is speaking of the New Creation.

He will recreate their spirit, or heart, as the term is synonymously used.

He says, "I will give them one heart." This suggests that a new kind of love is coming which will make them one as a body of people.

Jesus said, "That they may be one even as we are one."

In John 13:35-36 we read, "By this shall all men know that ye are my disciples, if ye have love one to another."

In the 36th chapter of Ezekiel, the 26th verse, we read, "A new heart also will I give you and a new spirit will I put within you."

Here is the prophecy of an absolutely New Creation.

He is going to take the stony heart of selfishness out of them, and give them His own heart of love.

11

In the 27th verse He says, "I will put my Spirit within you and cause you to walk in my statutes."

There will not only be a New Creation, but His Indwelling is promised.

We can hear Jesus saying, "He is with you, but He shall be in you."

I Peter 3:4 "But let it be the hidden man of the heart."

Here we are given a title for the recreated human spirit. He is called the "hidden man of the heart." He is the New Creation man. He is "the man."

The physical body is not the man, it is the temporary dwelling place for the man.

The reasoning faculties are not the man, they are his servants.

The body is the home of the five senses, or the five servants of the man. All of the knowledge that the reasoning faculties ever get comes through the five senses, or the five servants of the brain.

The brain would lie dormant, inactive, if the five senses did not function.

It would be good to note here that all of the knowledge that is taught in our colleges, universities and technical schools has come to man through these five channels.

The only way that man can obtain knowledge, or an education, is through these five servants, or members of the physical body.

Romans 7:22 "For I delight in the law of God after the inward man." Here this hidden man is called the "inward man." In either case, the "hidden man" is "the man."

The personality of the inner man is sometimes effected by the outer man.

2 Cor. 4:16 "Wherefore we faint not; but though our outward man is decaying, yet our inward man is renewed day by day."

Eph. 3:16 "That he would grant you, according to the riches of his glory, that ye may be strengthened with his ability in the inward man." (lit.)

The outward, or the visible man, is the one that you salute on the street.

The inward man is the one who gives this outer man either his attractiveness or his repulsiveness.

It is a very remarkable fact that God deals with the "inward man" instead of the outer man.

Spiritual things are unveiled to this "hidden man of the heart."

The Holy Spirit makes His home in the "hidden man."

Sin consciousness comes from this "inward man."

It is deeply important that you understand this fact: it is the recreated spirit that convicts of sin in the believer, and our conscience is his voice speaking to our reason.

We stated before that the "hidden man" is the part of us that is recreated, receives Eternal Life, and becomes a New Creation.

One of our recent translators gives 2 Cor. 5:17 like this, "Wherefore if any man is in Christ there is a new self brought into being, but old things have passed away, behold all things have become new."

The reconciliation it speaks of in the next verse is between this "hidden man of the heart" and the Father-God.

He never speaks of a reconciliation between the mind, or the reasoning faculties, and God, it is always a reconciliation of the heart.

When I first saw this truth unfolded, it began to have an effect upon my attitude toward some of the teachings that I had accepted in my early days.

Let us think of man as being in God's class. He is a spirit. He is an eternal spirit. He is capable of receiving the nature of God. He is capable of loving God. He is capable of becoming a son of God.

You understand, he was created in the image and the likeness of God, that is, spiritual likeness.

He lost that image in the Fall, but it is restored in the New Creation.

There is a very remarkable term used in the Pauline Revelation many times. For instance, in the first chapter of Ephesians it occurs (in one form or another) eleven or twelve times.

Take this as an illustration, Eph. 1:7 "In whom we have our Redemption."

Notice the first two words, "In whom," "in Christ," or "In Him."

For a long time that bothered me. I wondered what it meant.

I came upon something in John 15:5 that helped me. "I am the vine, and ye are the branches."

The branch is a part of the vine. The vine is a part of the branch. The two are one.

In Eph. 1:6 he says, "We are in the beloved."

In Eph. 2:6 it states, "We are seated together."

We are seated with this Beloved One at the Right Hand of the Father.

Eph. 2:6-7 "And raised us up with him, and made us to sit with him in the heavenly places in Christ Jesus: that in the ages to come he might show the exceeding riches of his grace in kindness toward us in Christ Jesus."

In Eph. 2:10 it tells us that "we are his workmanship created in Christ Jesus."

You see, this occured before the Resurrection of the Master.

When Christ was recreated the Father said, "This day have I begotten thee."

In the mind of Justice the entire Body of Christ was recreated.

This becomes a reality in us the moment we accept Christ as our Saviour and confess Him as our Lord. We then receive Eternal Life, the Nature of the Father. This makes us New Creations.

Now come back to the scripture I quoted, "Wherefore if any man is in Christ there is a new creation, a new self. The old things of the old self have passed away, behold, they have become new, and all these things are of God: who has reconciled us unto himself through Christ."

Romans 6:4-8 "We were buried therefore with him through baptism into death: that like as Christ was raised from the dead through the glory of the Father, so we also might walk in the newness of life."

Notice the next verse. "For if we have become united with him in the likeness of his death, we shall be also in the likeness of his resurrection: knowing this, that our old man was crucified with him, that the body of sin might be done away, that so we should no longer be in bondage to sin." Note the tense, "was" not "is."

"For he that hath died is justified from sin. But if we died with Christ, we believe that we shall also live with him."

Way's translation throws much light on this. "Well then, if that baptism made us share His death, it must have made us share His burial too. It must follow that, as Messiah was raised from among the dead by means of the descent of His Father's glory, so we too, who arose with Him, are to be employed wholly in the activities of the New Life.

"For if, by having died like Him, we have entered into living union with Him, most certainly we shall not be less so in consequence of having risen with Him. This we recognize, that our former self was nailed to His cross with Him, so that that body which was the instrument of sin might be made impotent for evil, so that we could not any longer be slaves of sin."

Notice carefully that the part of us that was recreated, made new, was "the hidden man of the heart." He is called "the old man."

This old man was crucified with Christ. It was neither our physical body nor our reasoning faculties, but our spirit. That is the part of us that was Spiritually Dead and had to be recreated.

Col. 3:9-10 "Seeing that ye have put off the old man with his doings, and put on the new man, that is being renewed unto knowledge after the image of him that created him."

Notice that the "old man" was put off, crucified with Christ.

When Christ arose from the dead a "new man" arose with Him. That new self is the human spirit.

Now the physical body, which is the home of the five senses, must be brought into conformity with Christ, who is the Head of the Body.

This brings us to Romans 12:1-2, "I beseech you therefore, brethren, by the mercies of God, to present your bodies a living sacrifice, holy, acceptable to God, which is your spiritual service."

"And be not fashioned according to this age: but be ye transformed (or transfigured) by the renewing of your mind, that ye may prove what is the good and acceptable and perfect will of God."

This body is the home, or dwelling place, of the spirit. This recreated human spirit wishes to communicate its new-found joy to those about it.

Hidden away as it is in the human body, it has no way of communication but through the five senses.

Therefore, the first thing that must be done after one is recreated is to bring these five senses into subjection to the recreated human spirit, and the Word. When this is done the mind will be renewed.

Although you are Born Again you still possess the same mind and body that had been under the dominion of the Adversary. This is the reason that it is so important to renew the mind and bring it into harmony with the recreated spirit.

You must bring it into subjection to this new self that has come into being.

The trouble with the majority of believers is that their minds have never been renewed.

The mind will never be renewed until they begin to practice love. They must live this love life that Jesus introduced to the world.

THE NEW KIND OF SELFISHNESS

"If any man be in Christ there is a New Creation." This New Creation is born of God, and God is love; so the New Creation is a Love Creation.

In our Redemption, Love went the limit. The cross and the three days of suffering was love's limit.

Now we are born of that Love; so we have become Love Creations.

We are partakers of Love's nature. We have the attributes of Love. God reproduces Himself in the New Creation. He makes a superman of Love that "seeks not his own." This New Creation is not provoked by persecution or by slander, or by anything that the people ruled by selfishness can do.

You see, the New Birth made a New Self, a New Spirit, a New Man; and it gives to man a new kind of selfishness. It is the selfishness manifested in Paul and the other members of that early organization called the Church. It plans to give more than it gets, and it is perfectly selfish in this struggle to give more than another can give.

It denies itself to give more. It is really Christ let loose in us.

You can hear the cry, "Master, You died for me. I live now for those for whom You died. You became a slave of love for me. I will become a love slave for them."

In 2 Cor. 5:13 we read, "For whether we are beside ourselves, it is unto God; or whether we are of sober mind, it is unto you. For the love of Christ constraineth us; because we thus judge, that one died for all, therefore all died; and he died for all, that they that live should no longer live unto themselves."

This Selfishness, as I love to call it, is the kind of love that sought the cross for me.

You remember that dear old saint, Polycarp, a convert of John the Beloved. When he was eighty-two, he started on that long trip to Rome, to confess before the Roman authorities that he was a love slave of Jesus Christ. They pled with him in every town through which he went on his way, that a stake and fagots awaited him. His heart was set on giving his testimony in Rome. When he arrived, he was arrested; they tried him, but he refused to recant. They tied him to the stake and heaped the fagots around him.

The authorities pled with him to blaspheme the Name. Tenderly he looked at them and said, "I have served this Master nearly eighty years. I love Him. He is my Lord." And then, with a firm voice he said, "Light your fire"; and in the midst of the flame he cried, "Father, forgive them, they know not what they do."

You could hear him say, "He loved me. He gave Himself up for me. If He gave Himself for me, it is no more than right that I should give myself for others."

It was love that led him. It is Love that leads the way of unselfishness.

Let us notice a basic fact: there are two great forces in the world, this new kind of Love (agapa) that Jesus brought, which springs out of the heart of the Father, and Selfishness, which is the nature of Satan.

Satan is spiritually dead. Spiritual death has given birth to Selfishness. Selfishness has dominated the human race.

Man is spiritually dead until he receives the nature of God.

Then, the combat in the world is between Eternal Life and Spiritual Death, or between Agapa and Selfishness.

The outstanding characteristic of natural man is Selfishness. It has given to us every one of the major sins that are destroying the human race.

Selfishness is the parent of the liquor traffic, gambling, and every other sin.

The husband who comes home half drunk doesn't love his family as much as he loves himself. The mother who has taken on the unhappy habits of modern society, and dares display these habits in the presence of her growing children, loves herself and her appetites more than she loves her children.

The natural man cannot love his children as much as he loves himself. He cannot love his wife as much as he loves himself.

The natural human heart is a partaker of the Satanic nature, Selfishness; and when that Selfishness gains the ascendancy it makes the man a despot in his home, filling it with the spirit of tyranny.

I saw a couple who had lived very unhappily and had thought much about separating, but there were little children. The father had a godly background, and so had the mother, but neither of them had ever received Eternal Life.

After the children came along, the wife began to feel the irritations of bondage and said, "These children just rob me of my liberty." The husband began to feel the same limitations. Selfishness began to grow apace. The home was not a home. It was just a place where they quarreled and made up, found fault, and cursed the children.

Then one day my little book, "The New Kind of Love," fell into the hands of the husband. He brought it home and started to read it. He became so engrossed in it that his wife wanted to know what he was reading.

You see, Selfishness is always jealous. The keener and richer your Selfishness is, the more sensitive you become.

She became very curious as to what that little book was.

Finally she said, "What is that you are reading?"

He said, "It is the most wonderful book I have ever read."

He laid it down on the table, and she began to read it. She hadn't read half of it before she made her decision. She had seen things.

When he came into the house she said, "How far did you read in that book?"

"Nearly   of it. One of the men at the office gave it to me." He responded. "What do you think of it?"

"I only wish we had gotten hold of it when we were first married and life would have been different," she said.

He picked up one of his children and held it in his arms. "Wife," he said, "would you like to go with me on this thing? I would like to have Eternal Life. I am sick of my selfishness."

She looked into his face, and reached out her hand and said, "My dear, I will go the whole way with you."

The two older children were not home when it happened, and the father and mother did not tell them about it.

Three or four days later the oldest girl said, "Mother, what has happened to you and Dad? You haven't quarreled since last week." Then the mother told the story to her, and the girl, in her mother's arms whispered, "Mother, I want it too."

And so, Love came to live in that house.

After a bit every member of the household sought to give the other more than he received. Love's rivalry began to develop. The husband and wife sought to out-do each other in love.

You see, when two New Creation people, Love filled, begin to practice Agapa, the very atmosphere of heaven is in that home.

Love's slogan is, "I am not seeking my own, but your happiness."

Wouldn't it be wonderful if we could have classes that would take up the study of Agapa. There has never been a chair of "Love" in any of our Colleges or Universities, and yet it is the most important thing in life.

You cannot adjust the labor and capital situation by law or by force. It can only be settled with Agapa.

Oh, if there should arise in the labor world a great leader who could evangelize the labor world and prove to them that Selfishness has never yet built anything that it did not destroy!

Sense Knowledge has built cities, but it always destroys them.

Few of us have recognized that there are two kinds of ambitions: one was born out of the desire to conquer and to reign, and to have and to hold, no matter what effect it had upon those who stand in the way; the other is the ambition to give, and to build, and to make happy; to educate and to train, and to make beautiful, glad homes. One is the Jesus kind, and the other is inspired by Satan.

You know, one of the sweetest things that Paul ever said was, "He counted me worthy to represent Love, even to represent God, to represent the new kind of love." Saul the hater, became Paul, the lover.

I wish that there could be little societies of men and women who would come together to study how to develop this new kind of love, so that they would have the new kind of selfishness.

I know a man and woman who lived very unhappily for nearly thirty years. They could not separate. They talked about it. They planned on it. They had even gone to their lawyer to talk it over; but when the real thing came, they could not seem to do it. They received a copy of my book, "The New Kind of Love," and then they came to my services and I happened to be speaking on this new kind of selfishness.

He came to see me a little while after that and said, "Do you know that my wife and I have found the thing we have been hunting for, for thirty years? We are playing the game now. Each one of us is trying to get the advantage of the other in love. Four or five of our neighbors have started to practice love also. One of them came the other night and said to me, 'You know, I can't practice this love. I don't have it in my heart,' and then my wife pointed her to the Lamb o. God; and now she has that new kind of love too."

Wouldn't it be wonderful if every one of you who read this book would become an evangel of this new kind of Love, this new kind of Selfishness?

We have seen the sons of Selfishness become the sons of Love. We have seen the old Selfishness meet this new kind of Selfishness and be defeated.

The great combat today is between Selfishness and Love. Satan is the symbol of Selfishness; Jesus is the symbol of Love.

Chapter The Third

LOVE AND SELFISHNESS . . . .
THE TWO GREAT SPIRITUAL FORCES IN THE WORLD

ERE are some things that love has never done: it has never enslaved the weaker; it never takes advantage of the ignorant; it has never reigned as a despot or tyrant; it did not vote for the rum traffic; it never steals or takes advantage; it never seeks a divorce; it is never in court as a criminal; it never seeks its own.

It never behaves unseemly in the family life; it never gets drunk; it never sets a bad example before the children; it does not swear, blaspheme, or use vile language; it does not remember evil that has been committed against it; it does not talk about the weakness and failure of others; it does not rejoice in evil things, and it is never happy when its enemy has been defeated.

This is the negative side of love.

You ask, "what does love do?"

It seeketh not its own; it destroys selfishness; it bears the burdens of others.

When it discovers that someone has done an unseemly thing, it covers it up, it shields it and never talks about it.

Can't you see the vast contrast between selfishness and love?

It is no wonder that the Commissar under Stalin who had charge of the educational system of Russia said, "We must kill love, we hate Christians. Love makes men soft. We must learn to hate. We must learn to kill."

That is selfishness unbridled. In a country where love has been destroyed, it becomes perfectly shameless.

Here are some facts we must recognize.

There are two kinds of love. One is natural human love, the other is the Jesus kind of love.

In the opening of this chapter I gave you a picture of the Jesus kind of love, the kind Communism hates. Why do they hate this love? Because Communism is builded upon selfishness.

21

You see, there are two kinds of Communism. There is a Communism governed by selfish men, and a Communism governed by love.

Following the birth of the early church there was such an outpouring of love that "they had all things in common, and no one said aught that he possessed was his own."

Satan has tried to imitate that through selfishness, through selfish men, but it cannot be done.

It is a notorious fact that there are only three or four million communists in Russia, and they are the rulers and under-rulers of the other one hundred and fifty or sixty million people.

The rulers believe in Communism because it makes them masters, and their people slaves.

No form of government where selfishness reigns is safe for the weak and poor.

Sense Knowledge governments have always enslaved the poor and weak. The strong govern the weak. Might is right in the realm of selfishness.

These selfish law makers fear the Jesus kind of love for two reasons.

In the first place, it reveals their meanness and selfishness. The other reason is that the Jesus kind of love is the positive enemy of selfishness. The two cannot work together.

You see, self preservation is the first law of natural man. It seeks to save itself, while love is the very opposite . . . it seeks to save others.

All the crimes that were committed in war, international crimes, were born of selfishness.

The war between labor and capital is a war of selfishness. Capital is builded upon selfishness.

Love would never go on strike.

Love would never grind labor's face into the dust.

The only solution of the labor and capital problem is to bring the capitalists into vital contact with Agapa, the new kind of Love.

This new kind of love is the nature of God, imparted to man in the New Birth.

It is the only solution of the labor and capital problem.

Selfishness of a deadly type is sweeping our land. It is bound to bring a war between capital and labor.

Capital has everything to lose in a war of that kind, and labor has nothing to gain. Labor is dependent upon capital for its living.

The only solution is the Jesus kind of love . . . the love that He brought to the world.

Selfishness has given birth to every ideology that is deadly.

Capital and organized labor is one of its fruitages.

One branch of labor says we must have Communism.

There can be no peace in the world as long as selfishness is ruling. There must arise a man of love, with the same ability to lead men as a Stalin or a Hitler, to lead the forces out of the realm of selfishness into the realm of love.

The love of what money gives is the root of all kinds of evil. When a selfish man gains the ascendancy in a community, he becomes a menace to society.

The Church is the only enemy of selfishness. When I say "Church," I mean the New Creation folk, the people who walk in love. Not the church as she is today. Many of the leaders of our denominations are modernists and even Communists.

Spiritual death, the nature of Satan, has given selfishness to us.

The nature and Life of the Son of God has given to us Love, and the conflict today is between Love and Selfishness.

Love awaits a leader, to build a new type of Christianity.

A new type of men, who will teach cooperation rather than exploitation.

It will either be that, or we will become the slaves of another Hitler.

As long as selfishness reigns, the strong will enslave the weak. The intellectual will enslave the ignorant. The classes will enslave the masses.

The French Revolution did not solve the problem of France. Stalin did not solve the Russian problem. Hitler did not solve the German problem.

We have one tremendous responsibility facing us, and that is prayer!

The only solution of the impending problem is to bring God on the scene.

We need a national Revival . . . . not a Revival of religion, but a Revival of Eternal Life.

Only Eternal Life will give us the New Love Law that should rule us.

Chapter The Fourth

THE SPIRIT OF MAN

OR years we were mystified as to the source of thoughts. We knew that they were not the children of reason. They flashed upon us, they came leaping at us from nowhere.

Beautiful melodies would float into our consciousness and gain the mastery over us; poetry would come, beautiful couplets, to which reason did not give birth.

Solutions of problems that had bothered us for days came to us unsought, unheralded.

Inventions and creative things flashed into our minds independent of Sense Knowledge sources.

Designs of beautiful structures, fabrics, and pictures that staggered reason came floating into the mind as clouds on a June day pass over our heads. From whence did they come?

Then we discovered Prov. 20:27, "The spirit of man is the lamp of Jehovah."

This spirit is to guide the reasoning faculties. So few enjoy the Lord's Lamp or take advantage of it.

We learned that man is a spirit. He is in the same class with God. He can live independently of the body. He is eternal.

We learned that there are two kinds of education, spirit education and mind education.

We discovered that the church and our educational system had never seriously attempted to understand the real man.

In the babe we see purely the physical. Then as the child's mind begins to reach out and becomes inquisitive, the child becomes simply mind and body to us.

We are careful to feed its body, to build it up, to train the mind and make it efficient, but who has ever taught or trained the spirit?

We heard much in psychological discussions about the sub-

25

conscious mind. At first we were thrilled with it. Then we discovered that it was nothing but our own spirit.

We found that conscience is the voice of the spirit, reason is the voice of our mind, and feelings are the voice of our body.

There are two kinds of consciences: one of the Christian, the child of God, and the other, the conscience of natural man.

We discovered that there are three kinds of spirit development.

Natural man can develop his spirit until it becomes a force in him. We see this in Christian Science, Unity, Spiritualism and other psychological religions. This is the natural, unregenerated human spirit being cultivated.

The human spirit is naturally very religious, because it is God-hungry. It is the mother of all human religions.

Christianity is God's answer to the hunger of the human spirit.

Every human religion attempts to answer this hunger and fails.

The part of man that is Born Again is the spirit. It receives the nature and Life of God.

It is our spirit that can contact God, or contact Satan. Reason cannot find God. Sense Knowledge has been unable to discover God, or the human spirit.

It can see evidences of a Creator, but it cannot find Him.

It can see evidences of man's spirit, but it cannot understand it or find it in the body.

Natural man's spirit is dominated largely by evil. Men have used it to gain the mastery over others for their own ends.

Then there are demonized spirits, men who are controlled by evil spirits. Oftentimes they perform prodigies, miracles, it seems.

The scriptures speak of this type: "Necromancers, spiritualists, and mediums." They are all demon-ruled spirits.

Often their minds have no part in what they say. Demons speak through their lips independent of Sense Knowledge.

These men can become deeply spiritual and become deep in the things of Satan.

The third kind of Spirituality is that of the New Creation spirit, for a man becomes a New Creation by receiving the Life and nature of God.

The Holy Spirit makes His home in the physical body and dominates the human spirit that has been recreated. As this is cultured and developed through the Word, there is no limit to its possibilities.

The effect of the spirit upon the body is little understood. It would pay materia medica to study this phase of healing.

Prov. 15:4 "A gentle tongue is a tree of life; but perverseness therein is a breaking of the spirit."

Words affect the human spirit. Your mind may cast aside the unkind words that are spoken, but your spirit absorbs them.

Prov. 15:13 "A glad heart maketh a cheerful countenance; But by sorrow of heart the spirit is broken." (The word "heart" is used interchangeably with the word "spirit.")

Job 19:2 "Then Job answered and said, How long will ye vex my soul, and break me in pieces with words?"

Words are more dangerous than bricks or stones. They are more potent than pen or brush. Bones they break not, but hearts they crush.

Prov. 17:22 "A cheerful heart is a good medicine; but a broken spirit drieth up the bones."

Prov. 18:14 "The spirit of a man will sustain his infirmity; but a broken spirit, who can bear it?"

In these scriptures we see the secret of healing for the body. We are praying for the sick daily. Every man who is sick physically, is sick in spirit; for the moment his spirit is healed, his body becomes well.

Our first ministry is to bring them in contact with the healing Word.

Psalms 107:20 "He sent His Word and healed them."

Matt. 8:8 The Centurion said to Jesus, "But speak the Word and my servant is healed." The Centurion recognized that Jesus healed folks with words.

You cannot heal bodies with words, but you can heal man's spirit with words. You heal the spirit, then the spirit heals the body.

It is the Logos on our lips that heals the spirit of sick men and women. The Word of God is the healer.

When we know how to rightly divide the Word, we will be able to administer the right kind of spiritual medicine, the right portion of scripture to the sick one to bring healing.

The secret of the divine life is to learn how to live in the spirit realm, how to have one's lamp filled with the oil of heaven, and to keep one's spirit fit so that no disease can break in upon it.

This brings before our minds the distinction between wisdom and knowledge.

Knowledge comes from reflection, observation, contact with people, books, and teachers.

Wisdom comes from one of two sources . . . . God or Satan.

James 3:13-18 "Who is wise and understanding among you? Let him show by his good life his works in meekness of wisdom. But if ye have bitter jealousy and faction in your heart, glory not and lie not against the truth. This wisdom is not a wisdom that cometh down from above, but is earthly, sensual, devilish. For where jealousy and faction are, there is confusion and every vile deed. But the wisdom that is from above is first pure, then peaceable, gentle, easy to be entreated, full of mercy and good fruits, without variance, without hypocrisy."

Here are the two kinds of wisdom in contrast.

We have two kinds of knowledge in contrast. We have the knowledge that comes from the Senses. We have this knowledge in our universities, colleges and technical schools; the knowledge we use every day in our factories, knowledge that seems to be independent of God, and often seeks to be independent of God.

The other kind of knowledge is Revelation Knowledge which comes from the Word.

Sense Knowledge is often at war with Revelation Knowledge.

Man needs Revelation Knowledge to complete his education.

Sense Knowledge cannot find God, know the reason for man, the reason for Creation, the source of Life, or the source of motion.

When it faces problems of this kind, it turns speculative and forms theories.

Darwin's theory of evolution is a masterpiece of guessing. He went as far as Sense Knowledge could go, then he boarded an airplane of fancy, left the realm of facts, and wrote a book of speculations and theories. It has damned millions, but helped no one.

God imparts His message to your spirit.

The thing called "a hunch," that "still small voice," is your spirit, and is sometimes called "conscience."

The only way to know God and the Lord Jesus Christ is through the spirit.

I used to be confused when people would say, "If I could see some one healed, I would believe."

One of these skeptics happened to be with me when a man who had been bedfast was miraculously healed. His legs had refused to function. He was healed instantaneously. He walked and praised God. My friend said, "Well, that's all right, but it was his time to get well anyway."

Sense Knowledge cannot understand miracles. Only the spirit can reveal them.

When people come to our services, see men and women healed, and miracles performed, it gives them Sense Knowledge faith in healing. Many of them take their healing because of what they see and hear. But, if the trouble returns, as the adversary would doubtless make it, they would have no foundation, no root. They have no deep, rich knowledge of the Word.

They are like the seed that was sown in shallow soil. When the heat came, it died, for it had no deep root system.

Before a person can be permanently helped, his spirit must be educated in the Word of God.

Creative faith, Dominating faith, Healing faith, and Saving faith, are all in the spirit.

Faith is not a product of reason.

Sense Knowledge has never produced the kind of faith of which we are speaking. It can produce Sense Knowledge faith that believes in what it sees, hears and feels.

Love is the fruit of the spirit. (This does not refer to the Holy Spirit, but to the recreated human spirit.)

Gal. 5:16 is a wonderful exposition of the human spirit: "But I say, Walk by the spirit, and ye shall not fulfill the lust of the flesh (senses). For the flesh (or senses) lusteth against the spirit, and the spirit against the flesh (senses); for these are contrary the one to the other; that ye may not do the things that ye would."

In the 19th and 20th verses, he tells us about the works of the Senses, or the manifestations of the Senses.

The 22nd verse gives the fruits of the renewed human spirit. They are "love, joy, peace, longsuffering, kindness, goodness, faithfulness, meekness, self-control; against such there is no law. And they that are of Christ Jesus have crucified the flesh (or senses) with the passions and the lusts thereof."

When the human spirit gains the mastery over the Senses, it brings them into captivity. Then a man says, "I cannot do that. My conscience (which is the voice of his recreated spirit) will not permit it." His spirit has gained the mastery over his mind.

The mind in turn gains the mastery over the body, and brings the body into subjection to the mind.

"If we live by the spirit, let us by the spirit also walk." That is the human spirit.

Romans 8:1-3 deals with the same problem.

Third verse, "For what the law could not do, in that it was weak through the flesh (senses), God, sending His own Son in the likeness of sinful flesh (senses) and for sin, condemned sin in the flesh." (or senses).

What sin is condemned in our flesh? It is not sin of conduct as we understand, it is sickness.

Sin, here, is a broken law of the senses. Disease is condemned in the body.

Until you recognize that disease is an outlaw, and until your spirit grasps this fact, you will never build a fence against physical distress and disease.

When you realize that physical disease is an outlaw, and you still consort with that disease by pampering it, you are joining forces with the outlaw, and it will bring you under condemnation.

The 4th verse, (literal trans.) "That the righteous requirements of the law might be fulfilled in us, who walk not after the senses, but after the spirit. For they that are after the senses mind the things of the flesh (senses); but they that are after the spirit, the things of the spirit. For the mind of the flesh (senses) is death;

but the mind of the spirit is life and peace: because the mind of the senses is enmity against God; for it is not subject to the law of God, neither indeed can it be."

He is not speaking of the Holy Spirit, but of this recreated spirit and its place in your physical body.

Romans 12:1-2 "I beseech you therefore, brethren, by the mercies of God, to present your bodies a living sacrifice, holy, acceptable to God, which is your spiritual service. And be not fashioned according to this world; but be ye transformed by the renewing of your mind, that ye may prove what is the good and acceptable and perfect will of God."

The body, here, is brought into subjection to a renewed mind, and the renewed mind is brought into subjection to a recreated spirit.

Until your spirit gains the mastery over your senses, your faith will never be strong and vigorous.

Because "the spirit of man is the lamp of Jehovah," God, Himself must fill the lamp with oil of the right grade and from the right source. This oil is Eternal Life.

The lamp sheds light in the spirit realm, the realm of faith and the realm of love. It throws light upon the Word.

"Thy Word is a lamp unto my feet, and a light unto my pathway."

Your spirit is in the realm of creative faith, of dominating faith, faith that rules demons and disease.

I have found in my dealings with the sick during the early days of my ministry, that certain diseases filled me with fear. I shrank from going into their presence. I had seen their devastating work in my own family. But later I came to see that disease was not physical but spiritual.

When my spirit had fed upon the Word until it had developed a robust, unconscious faith, then I walked into the presence of diseases as a master.

Jesus' dominion was not a physical or mental dominion. He ruled men, the laws of nature, demons, and sickness by His spirit.

He said, "The words that I speak are not mine, but my Father's; and the works that I am doing are not mine, but my Father's."

John 6:63 "It is the spirit that giveth Life; the flesh (senses) profiteth nothing: the words that I have spoken unto you are spirit, and are life."

God is a spirit, Jesus is a spirit. He was here in a physical body so that men could see Him. His lips spoke Words of the Spirit.

When you give your spirit right-of-way, and it assumes the dominion in your life, love will be natural. Love is the fruit of the spirit.

When your spirit is recreated, that love will be the Jesus kind of love.

The natural man has natural love which is selfish, and turns to hatred, jealousy and ofttimes to murder.

The Jesus kind of love flows from the fountain of a recreated spirit.

John 6:47 "He that believeth hath Eternal Life." Eternal Life is the nature of God. That nature has now come into man's spirit.

1 John 5:13 "These things have I written unto you, that ye may know that ye have Eternal Life, even unto you that believe on the name of the Son of God."

1 John 4:8 "He that loveth not knoweth not God; for God is love."

1 John 3:14-17 "He that loveth not abideth in death. Whosoever hateth his brother is a murderer: and ye know that no murderer hath Eternal Life abiding in him."

Eternal Life abides in a man's spirit. When a man is recreated, and filled with the nature of the Father, which is love, there will come forth from his spirit love acts, promptings for love words and love deeds.

Let us study it from another angle.

The animal world acts by instinct. They have souls; they reason; they have affection. They have the power of choice in a measure, but instinct rules them.

God did their thinking for them. The animal's safety depends upon instinct. Sight and hearing have a second place.

When the wild animal trusts his sight or his hearing and ignores his instinct, he becomes a prey of his enemy.

When we ignore the voice of the recreated human spirit, we become a prey of the adversary.

1 Cor. 2:14 "Now the natural man receiveth not the things of the Spirit of God; for they are foolishness unto him; and he cannot know them, because they are spiritually understood."

The 13th verse, "Which things also we speak, not in words which man's wisdom teacheth, but which the spirit teacheth; combining spiritual things with spiritual words."

It is spiritual teaching. God's Spirit through the Word is teaching our spirits.

Natural man cannot know God.

Sense Knowledge has never been able to find God. Sense Knowledge makes man more skeptical. Ofttimes, the more Sense Knowledge a man possesses, the farther away he is from the Word.

2 Cor. 5:7 "We walk by faith, and not by sight."

Faith rules the spiritual man. Why? Because Jesus is the Lord and head of this New Man. The Word rules him.

It is deeply important that we realize that this New Creation has a law all its own.

John 13:34-35 "A new commandment I give unto you, that ye love one another; even as I have loved you, that ye also love one another. By this shall all men know that ye are my disciples, if ye have love one for another."

The New Creation has a priesthood of its own. Jesus is our High Priest. We New Creation folk belong to the Holy Priesthood. We have the joy of functioning in the Royal Priesthood.

1 Peter 2:5 "Ye also, as living stones, are built up a spiritual household, to be a holy priesthood, to offer up spiritual sacrifices, acceptable to God through Jesus Christ."

God has become our actual Father. We are His actual sons and daughters.

1 John 3:2-3 "Beloved, now are we the sons of God."

It is well that we know that reason and feelings, and the senses, are generally opposed to our spirit.

Some believers have never learned to live in their spirit. They live in their senses, their bodies largely ruling them.

Others live in their soul, or their intellect. They are what Paul calls, "psychic men."

1 Cor. 2:14 (marginal rendering) "Now the psychical (or natural) man receiveth not the things of the Spirit of God: for they are foolishness unto him; and he cannot know them, because they are spiritually understood."

A carnal believer is a baby believer who has been fed with milk, and not with meat.

1 Cor. 3:1-4 "And do ye not walk after the manner of men?"

This is one of the most striking sentences in that wonderful Epistle. This man, who is recreated, has never yet learned to walk in his spirit, governed by the Word. He walks as a common man. He walks just as he walked before he was Born Again.

In a short time, he will break fellowship with the Father and fall back again into the old life; a recreated man, but one dominated by the physical body, or his senses.

The New Creation man is to walk by faith.

Heb. 10:38 "But my righteous one shall live by faith: and if he shrink back, my soul hath no pleasure in him."

Shrink back from what? From the walk in the spirit by faith.

He shrinks back into a sense knowledge walk.

You can see, that if you are a recreated spirit, you should live in the realm of the spirit.

Matt. 4:4 "Man shall not live by bread alone, but by every word that proceedeth out of the mouth of God."

This righteous, recreated man lives by the Word, feeding on it, and obeying it.

We have found that man is a spirit being. God's dealings with him are through his spirit.

If he is sick, his spirit must be healed.

If he is ruled by sin, his spirit must be cleansed.

If his mind has not been renewed, the spirit does not have liberty or freedom, and cannot manifest Christ in his life.

The spirit of man is really the lamp of Jehovah.

Chapter The Fifth

THE FRUITS OF THE SPIRIT

E are not dealing with mysticism, philosophy or metaphysics. We are dealing with realities.

It is not something that the human reason has wrought out through observation or physical sensations, but we are dealing with the basic laws of man's being, the great spiritual laws that govern the unseen forces of life.

There are several great forces that emanate from the recreated human spirit.

They are to the spirit realm what iron, copper, gold and other metals are to the mechanical realm.

FAITH

The first force of the recreated human spirit is faith.

Faith is not the product of reason. It is the babe that is born in the human spirit.

God is a faith Spirit. He brought the universe into being by faith. He created the metals, gases, oils, and all that goes to make up the physical world, by faith.

By faith He brought the stars, sun and moon into being, as an artist brings a colorful landscape to life upon a drab canvas.

He is a faith God. He works by faith. As recreated men and women, we are to work and live by faith.

Jesus said, "If a man had faith as a grain of mustard seed, he could say to yonder mountain, 'Up, be hurled into the sea,' and the mountain would obey him."

We know that the sea, the wind, the fish, and the laws of nature obeyed the faith voice of the Son of God.

We know that reason did not govern Jesus, but His Spirit, which is above reason, ruled, for Jesus did the most unreasonable things.

He stood by the tomb of the rotting body of Lazarus and said to that body, "Lazarus, come forth," and the spirit of Lazarus

35

came from Paradise, entered into that physical body and it was renewed, made perfectly normal and healthy, by faith.

It was the voice of faith. Words filled with faith dominated the laws of death, and subdued the forces that have ruled the human since the fall of man.

It was the same voice that spoke to the water and it became wine. It was the same voice that said to the sea, "Peace, be still."

When one realizes the source of faith, then he will be able to develop it. When one learns what produces faith, the kind of food and activities that are necessary to develop it, he has arrived.

Faith is a product of your spirit, just as wisdom is a product of your spirit; faith is developed and wisdom is enriched by meditation in the Word of God.

This Word came to man through the human spirit, God communicating it to man's reasoning faculties. Man's spirit was governed by God's spirit, enabling him to bring God's message to man's consciousness through this Revelation.

By the same token, faith is developed in the human spirit by the Word of God. It comes by acting on the Word.

That is your exercise. Every time you act upon the Word, faith becomes stronger. You could lie in bed until your limbs lose their ability to bear the rest of your body. So it is with faith, it must be continually exercised in order to develop it.

RIGHTEOUSNESS

There is a second fact that must be clearly apprehended, that is Righteousness. Man remains a prisoner of sin consciousness until the Righteousness fact becomes a living reality in his spirit.

There can be no development of faith as long as sin consciousness dominates the human spirit.

We will not be able to exercise God's wisdom in our daily walk if sin consciousness dominates our spirit.

It is an unhappy fact that the church, instead of destroying sin consciousness with the truth, has developed sin consciousness by preaching sin.

If they had preached the cure of sin consciousness, if they had made clear the fact that man received Eternal Life, and that Eternal Life was the nature of God, and that the nature of God is Righteousness, man would begin to depend upon that new kind of Righteousness that has been imparted to him.

He would say this: "If I am a New Creation, created in Christ Jesus, I must be a Righteous creation. If I am a new man, I must be free from the bondage of the old man. What He says about Righteousness of the New Creation is true. Then my spirit is Righteous. If it is Righteous, then I can stand in the Father's presence without fear of judgment or condemnation.

"There is therefore now no condemnation to me, because I am in Christ Jesus, a New Creation, created in Righteousness and holiness and truth."

That very fact solves the whole problem of our enjoying the riches of the fulness of our Redemptive rights in Christ.

I am not afraid to act, because I know that all that Christ wrought, He wrought for me. His entire substitutionary work, from the time He was made sin until He sat down at the right hand of the Father, was all for me.

He did nothing for Himself.

If the New Creation is a result of the work that Christ wrought, the New Creation must be satisfactory to the Father.

If God is able, on the grounds of the Substitutionary work of Christ, to impart to man His nature, His very substance and being, and do it on legal grounds, then this man, who has received the substance and nature of God can stand in God's presence just as though sin had never been.

Now we can see the vast possibilities of this recreated spirit. It actually enters into a limitless life.

The human mind and body begin to lose their place of dominance in our consciousness, and the spirit comes to the front and actually begins to take over the rest of the man. It has been held a prisoner through all the ages, now it is set free.

Its blind eyes at last are opened. Its paralyzed limbs are at last filled with life. Its voice now becomes the voice of God.

Just as soon as you realize the reality of your Righteousness in Christ, you are emancipated, for Righteousness is the emancipator.

Righteousness is your Redemption in Christ. Satan has no

dominion over the man who knows he is the Righteousness of God in Christ.

How masterful this makes Christianity!

There can be no perfect coordination between your spirit and your reasoning faculties until you recognize the reality of your spirit Redemption, your spirit Righteousness, and your spirit union with God.

WISDOM

It does not make any difference how much knowledge one has if he does not know how to use it.

It goes without argument that there is enough knowledge given in a Bible Institute or Theological Seminary to make any minister a success. It is a self-evident fact, however, that the majority of them are failures. Their followers are not instructed in Righteousness. They are continually seeking to be made holy and to have faith.

1 Cor. 1:30 tells us that Jesus was made unto us wisdom.

You see, wisdom is the ability to use knowledge so that it will be a blessing to the hearer.

Col. 1:9 gives us a sample of Paul's prayers, "That you may be filled with the knowledge of his will in all spiritual wisdom and understanding."

That is a remarkable statement, "in all wisdom and all understanding."

No College can give wisdom. There is no chair of wisdom in any University.

There are but two sources of wisdom, one from Satan and one from God.

James tells us in James 3:15, "This wisdom is not a wisdom that cometh down from above, but it is earthly, sensual and devilish."

The other wisdom comes down from above, and has all of the characteristics that adorned the life of Jesus. This wisdom belongs to every child of God.

James, in speaking of it, said, "If any man lacketh wisdom let him ask of God."

He is speaking of the babes in Christ.

Paul is writing to the full grown believer.

This wisdom is available for every crisis of life, just as His strength, His grace and love are available.

This wisdom really grows out of love. It is love at work in your daily life.

I look upon wisdom as the rarest gift that love brought with Redemption.

LOVE

Christianity is love in our daily contact with people. It is my acting as Jesus would in my place.

1 John 4:7-8 "Beloved, let us love one another; for love is of God; and every one that loveth is begotten of God, and knoweth God. He that loveth not knoweth not God; for God is love."

Jesus brought a new kind of love. He demonstrated it in His daily walk.

If He had control of one, love would dominate in all that he said and did. It would be the Father actually taking us over, living His own life through us.

The Holy Spirit's real ministry is building the Father's nature into us.

If we were doers of love, we could never be failures. We would never injure anyone knowingly. It would eliminate selfishness from our conduct. It would make us Jesus-like in our thinking, planning and doing.

There are no broken homes where love rules. There are no broken hearts and wrecked lives.

This new kind of love brings Him on the scene, making Him one with us in all that we are and do.

We have caught a glimpse of the Big Four of the Fruits of the Spirit.

There are many other fruits of the spirit, but I am convinced that they grow out of love. They are a part of the Father's love nature imparted to us in the New Creation.

Let love have its perfect work in your life. Measure all ambitions with this yardstick of love. Plan your life with the love nature of God dominating it.

Our Union With Deity

It is thrilling to know that man is in the same class of being with God, and that he may become a partaker of His Divine Nature. He may actually become a child of the Creator of the Universe.

The Father's Nature imparted to a man brings him into vital union with Deity.

Man is a spirit being, he has a soul, and he lives in a physical body. God calls this body His temple. It is His Holy of Holies now on earth.

We have never majored the fact of a man becoming a partaker of the Divine Nature. There has been no serious attempt to cultivate this recreated spirit.

We know that the part of man that is recreated and receives the nature of God is his spirit. You remember that Jesus said, "I am the vine and ye are the branches." That statement goes with Eph. 2:10, "For we are his workmanship, created in Christ Jesus." We grow out of Christ.

1 John 4:4 "Ye are of God my little children."

1 John 3:2 "Beloved, now are we children of God."

These scriptures prove one fact, that we came out of the womb of Omnipotence, and that our spirit, the real man, is born of God. God imparts to this man His own Nature.

I believe that this is the genius of Christianity.

You see, when one is recreated it does not mean that his mind is changed. His reasoning faculties may be governed by the same forces as before.

You understand that all the knowledge that the brain receives comes through the five senses. If a man is governed by his senses his spirit is held captive.

The New Creation should be ruled by the spirit, making it possible for him to have fellowship with the Father. His recreated spirit should rule his reasoning faculties.

Here are some facts: it is our spirit that is redeemed; the redemption of our bodies comes at the return of our Lord; Satan's dominion was broken over the spirit of man. Man has been freed from Satan's thrall. The senses are to be dominated by the recreated spirit.

When the senses are brought into subjection it means that the body is brought into subjection.

The term flesh, as used in Paul's Epistles, should almost invariably be translated senses. If this were done it would clear up much that we have failed to understand.

The combat mentioned in Gal. 5:16-26 would be a combat between the recreated spirit and the senses. He says, "Walk by the spirit," that means the recreated spirit, "and you will not fulfill the desires of the senses."

You see, the recreated spirit and the senses are constantly warring.

"But if you are led by the spirit," that is not the Holy Spirit, that is the recreated spirit, "ye are not under the law." The men under the law were led entirely by their senses.

In the New Creation the spirit is made righteous, it finds a new freedom in the presence of God and the Word. The Word no longer condemns, but it comforts. The Holy Spirit no longer convicts, but He leads the recreated spirit into the realities of His Redemption in Christ.

This recreated spirit now finds joy in the Word, and in fellowship with the Holy Spirit and the Father. It begins to feed on the Word. Before it was recreated it could not do this. The Word becomes spiritual milk for the New Creation.

Fruit-Bearing Branches

Now we come to one of the most remarkable features of the New Creation's life. It is the fruit bearing of the recreated spirit. The fruits he is to bear are the fruitage of the Vine.

Now you can understand John 15:5, "I am the vine, and ye are the branches." We are the fruit bearing part of the Vine. Jesus does not bear fruit. The Holy Spirit does not bear fruit. The branches bear the fruit, enabled by the Holy Spirit.

Now we come to Gal. 5:22, "But the fruit of the Spirit is love." I always thought that to mean the fruit of the Holy Spirit; the translators evidently thought the same thing, but that is not true. The word spirit should not have been capitalized, for it is the recreated spirit that is the fruit bearer. It is the branch of the vine that bears the fruit.

Romans 5:5 tells us the nature of these first fruits. "For the love of God is shed abroad in our hearts by the Holy Spirit." That means that the love of God comes with the New Birth to the human spirit (which is called the heart).

The first fruitage of the recreated spirit is love.

The strange new word that Jesus evidently coined is used, *agapa.*

You remember in 1 John 4:8 that God is called agapa, "God is love."

Now the recreated spirit is bearing the fruits of love.

"We know that we have passed from death into life because we love the brethren." Agapa is used here also. In this same chapter he says, "Let us not agapa in words only, but in deed and in truth."

You remember that the law of the New Covenant, which takes the place of the Old Covenant and its law is, "A new commandment I give unto you, that ye agapa one another even as I have agapaed you."

The law of the first Covenant was summed up by Jesus. The law was that a man should "love God with all his heart and his neighbor as himself."

Natural man could not love God. He might love some idea he had of God, as some of our modern preachers do today. The natural man cannot love or know God. He was to love his neighbor as himself. This too was an impossibility.

The New Covenant law says that we are to love "even as" Jesus loved us. Jesus loved my neighbor enough to suffer the torments of the damned for him. I am to love him the same way.

Jesus loved the world enough to go to hell for it. Paul said, speaking of his relations, "For I could wish that I myself were anathema from Christ." In other words, he said, "I love my brethren enough to go to hell for them. I would willingly be lost eternally if I could only lead them into the joy of this union with Christ."

You see, Paul had received this revelation truth of love, and it had taken possession of him. His heart was captured by it.

This revelation of the Father's nature being imparted to man is the genius of Redemption.

This new kind of love is the solution of every problem.

You understand that there was no love before Christ came. Women were bought and sold among all peoples. A woman had no standing until Christ gave her one. Up until 1840 men questioned whether or not a woman should have an education.

Slavery could not be abolished until love gained the supremacy in a man's heart.

The great forces in the world today are spiritual. They are greater than the Atom Bomb or the Hydrogen Bomb. They are greater than any of man's organizations. These two forces are the New Kind of Love and the Old Kind of Selfishness.

The labor and capital problems can only be settled by the law of the New Covenant. You see, this new law of love is the nature of God in practice. It is Eternal Life dominating the reasoning faculties. That is the reason it is so difficult to put it over in our land.

Selfishness has arisen to its supreme heights in both the economical and political worlds. The church has lost its dominion. No one cares much for its voice any more.

Our broken homes proclaim aloud that selfishness is the goddess of the divorce court. Many parents look upon children as a hindrance to their selfish happiness.

Few have ever recognized the Lordship of Jesus. His Lordship is our ticket into God's family. That Lordship really means the Lordship of Love. It is love gaining the ascendancy over the recreated spirit.

When a man receives Eternal Life, love becomes supreme in his life.

The recreated spirit is a product of love. It is born of God, and God is love. When it came forth, fresh from the womb of the Spirit, it was filled with the love nature of the Father.

If one allowed love to dominate him, we would see Jesus men and women facing selfishness, hatred and jealousy as the Master faced it during His earth walk.

Joy

Perhaps one of the richest fruits of the recreated spirit is joy. Joy is the evangel to a selfish world.

Joyful Christians have always been a challenge to a broken-hearted world.

Selfishness never gives joy, it gives only limited happiness. Happiness is the product of our surroundings. It is the satisfying of our senses. The material things that bring a man happiness may be taken from him in a moment and he is left desolate.

Joy belongs to the spiritual realm just as happiness belongs to the sense realm.

In John 15:11 Jesus said, "These things have I spoken unto you that my joy may be in you and your joy may be made full."

Jesus could have had but little happiness. His joy in people must have all been by faith.

He believed that He could meet the claims of Justice and conquer Satan. He believed that He could make the New Creation a possibility and that He could restore this lost, broken man to the heart of the Father. Thus He could say, "that my joy may be in you, and that your joy may be made full."

I linger over that sentence. I wondered what it would mean if a man could have his joy made full. It would be necessary that he become Jesus like, so that he could say, "For I do always the things that are pleasing to Him."

He could say as the Master said, "My meat is to do the will of Him who sent me."

Joy would be in knowing the Father's will and doing it.

John 16:22 and 24, "And ye therefore now have sorrow: but I will see you again, and your heart shall rejoice, and your joy no one taketh away from you." That was a promise and a prophecy.

The disciples had no joy. They could not have it until their spirits were recreated.

In the 24th verse He says, "Hitherto have ye asked nothing in my name: ask, and ye shall receive, that your joy may be made full."

This is the secret, then. He speaks of a fulness of joy. The first was that it might be made full. The means to make it full had not yet come into being. Here again He uses the strange expression, "that your joy may be made full."

He has given you the right to use His Name. It is really the Power of Attorney. We are to receive things from the Father;

He is going to do things for us as sons because we are using the Name of Jesus.

In the 23rd verse (marginal rendering) we read, "In that day ye shall ask me nothing. Verily, verily, I say unto you, if ye shall ask anything of the Father he will give it you in my name."

He practically forbids you to pray to Him, but we are to address our prayers to the Father in His Name, then our joys will be made full. How? By the answers that the Father gives.

John 17:13 "But now I come to thee; and these things I speak in the world, that they may have my joy made full in themselves."

Once more He uses this strange term of our having a fulness of joy. This time He is asking the Father that it might become a reality in us, and we know that His prayer was heard. We have a right to expect joy. It is something that the world cannot take from us.

Neither persecution nor torture could rob the disciples of their joy. Every martyr that we know anything about met death with a joy filled heart.

1 Peter 1:8 "Whom not having seen ye love; on whom, though now ye see him not, yet believing ye rejoice greatly with joy unspeakable and full of glory."

This must ever remain as the masterpiece of descriptive truth of the New Creation who has "joy unspeakable and full of glory." It is a joy that is beyond words.

This joy belonged to those early Saints. It was because of this joy, so apparent in the lives of the Christians, that the Prince of Madagascar accepted Christ. His mother, the Queen, had ordered all those confessing Christ to be flung to their death off a high precipice. The Crown Prince stepped forward, bowed low, and made his confession of faith in Christ. It was the unmistakable joy of the Christians that had touched the heart of the young Prince. He could not resist it. He accepted Christ and offered himself as a martyr.

Neh. 8:10 " . . . for the joy of Jehovah is your strength."

Isa. 35:10 is another picture of joy. "And the ransomed of Jehovah shall return, and come with singing into Zion; and everlasting joy shall be upon their heads; they shall obtain gladness and joy, and sorrow and sighing shall flee away."

Psalms 16:11 is a picture of the Master Himself after His Resurrection. "Thou wilt show me the path of life: In thy presence is fulness of joy; In thy right hand there are pleasures for evermore."

This is a photograph of the Master on that first Easter morn.

When a Believer is not joyful it is either because of broken fellowship or a lack of knowledge of what He is in Christ and what Christ is in him. He does not know what he is to the Father and what the Father can be to him. He has never entered into his inheritance in Christ.

It is vastly important that we know about our inheritance, that is, our present tense inheritance.

It is this unspeakable joy which makes you triumphant over the petty trials of life, and a victor over the trials that may come up.

PEACE

My heart looks upon this fruit of the New Creation as one of the most valuable.

You remember that Jesus said, "Peace I leave with you; my peace I give unto you; not as the world giveth, give I unto you. Let not your heart be troubled, neither let it be fearful."

John 16:33 "These things have I spoken unto you, that in me ye may have peace. In the world ye have tribulation: but be of good cheer; I have overcome the world."

What is peace? Why, it is the child of love.

When one comes to know his Father and know his place in Christ, and to know that Jesus is what the Word declares Him to be, he can repeat, "Jesus is my Shepherd Lord, I shall not fear what man may attempt to do unto me."

In the quietness of his heart he whispers, "My Father is greater than all. He loves me as He loved Jesus in His earth walk."

Then he whispers that marvelous scripture, John 14:23, "If a man love me he will keep my word and the Father and I will love him and we will come and make our home with him." Can anything equal that promise?

When the heart knows beyond a shadow of a doubt that the Father and Jesus are making their home in your home, you have a feeling of safety that no earthly or demoniacal power can destroy.

You have the "peace of God which passeth all understanding."

You are anchored in the spirit realm of love now.

Phil. 4:6,7 becomes a reality. "In nothing be anxious, but in everything by prayer and supplication with thanksgiving, let your requests be made known unto God."

I have been invited to come boldly to the throne of Grace, the throne of love gifts. I know that whatsoever I ask of the Father in Jesus' Name I will receive. Because of this I have no anxiety.

I have entered into His rest. Why? The next verse tells us. "And the peace of God which passeth all understanding shall guard your hearts and thoughts in Christ Jesus."

Your heart is safe-guarded. Your thoughts are safe-guarded.

1 Peter 5:7 "Casting all your anxiety upon him, because he careth for you."

Where there is anxiety there is no peace, and where there is no peace, there is no rest. Now we have entered into His protective care, it is the realm of His rest. This belongs to every believer.

When one fails to have peace, quietness, and rest of spirit he has either broken fellowship with the Father, or he does not enjoy the riches of his relationship with Him.

He has not taken advantage of the Holy Spirit's ministry. That ministry is to build the Word into your spirit consciousness until you lose all sin consciousness. He will build into you a Father consciousness and a child consciousness. You will become aware of His protective care and love.

Now you can understand what the prophet meant when he said, "Great peace have they who love thy law, and nothing shall offend them."

Isa. 26:31 is a beautiful prophecy of this strange thing called peace. "Thou wilt keep him in perfect peace whose mind is stayed on thee, because he trusteth in thee."

LONGSUFFERING

This fruit of the spirit in the heart of a believer is really love's nursery. The Believer is now suffering with the selfish ones, perhaps loved ones. You see, we are living in a world dominated by selfishness.

We are the Jesus folk, and we are to love those selfish ones as He loved them. We are taking His place, acting in His stead. He came to destroy the works of the Adversary.

The longsuffering believers are partners of the Master in this great work.

You will never be free from selfish men and women; they are the burdens that you have to bear. They are always crying for their share. They want, they demand, and they will fight to gratify their senses. The longsuffering ones must bear with them. We must suffer for a long time with the babes.

This is love's ministry, suffering with the babes in Christ.

Paul tells about them in 1 Cor. 3:1-3, "And I, brethren, could not speak to you as unto spiritual, but as unto babes in Christ. I fed you with milk, not with meat; for ye were not yet able to bear it; nay, not even now are ye able: for ye are yet carnal: for whereas there is among you jealousy and strife, are ye not carnal, and do ye not walk after the manner of men?"

This is an unhappy picture; but it is true, and the deeply spiritual men and women must bear the burdens of these babes.

Heb. 5:12 gives you another picture. "For when by reason of time ye ought to be teachers, ye have need again that someone teach you the rudiments of the first principles of the oracles of God; and are become such as have need of milk, and not of solid food."

Notice, "when by reason of time ye ought to be teachers." They should be grown up in the Word and helping others, but they are still babes.

You who are strong must bear the infirmities of the weak. You must take the Master's place.

They will be selfish. They will criticize you. They may lie about you. They are often the scandal-mongers of the church. They see evil instead of good. Their ears are open to the senses.

But you, you have grown to the full stature of a man or woman in Christ, and must bear with them and be patient and kind.

Chapter The Sixth

DEVELOPING YOUR SPIRIT LIFE

E know that wisdom comes from the human spirit, and that God's impartation of wisdom does not come direct to the intellect, but through the human spirit to the intellect.

Millions of dollars have been spent in developing the human body, and hundreds of millions have been spent in developing the human mind; but the real man, which is the spirit, has been utterly neglected.

We had thought that the only way to develop it was through religion; but when we realize that the great forces of humanity are spiritual, and that they all emanate from the spirit, then it becomes vitally important that this part of man be seriously considered.

Jesus promised cooperation with our spirits after He had settled the sin problem and sat down at the right hand of the Father.

John 14:16-17 is a sample of His promises, "And I will make request of the Father, and He shall give you another Comforter, that He may be with you forever, even the Spirit of Truth: whom the world cannot receive; for it beholdeth Him not, neither knoweth Him: ye know Him; for He abideth with you, and shall be in you."

This Spirit of truth was the Holy Spirit, and He was to come and take Jesus' place after He had finished His Redemptive work.

It is almost an unknown fact that the Holy Spirit does not communicate knowledge to the intellect, except in rare cases where one is so dense spiritually that He must communicate with the senses.

All the knowledge that natural man has, has come through the senses. It may be necessary that the Spirit come to man's level (his senses) in order to deal with him.

John 16:13 "Howbeit when he, the Spirit of truth, is come, he shall guide you into all the truth: for he shall not speak from himself; but what things soever he shall hear, these shall he speak."

This promise was not only for the special revelation that God

49

gave to us through the Apostle Paul, but it is for every believer.

He is to guide us into the reality of the Redemptive work of Christ. All that Christ wrought in His Substitution was wrought in His Spirit. It was His Spirit that was made sin. It was His Spirit that suffered the torments of judgment on the behalf of humanity.

It was His Spirit that was declared righteous. He was made alive in His Spirit.

It was His Spirit Resurrection rather than His physical Resurrection that has given to humanity its Redemption.

Man is so tied up with Sense Knowledge that he has only seen the physical suffering of Christ on the cross, and His physical Resurrection.

It was something infinitely beyond that. It was His Spirit that was suffering for our spirits.

It was His Spirit that was made Righteous for our spirits. It was His Spirit that was recreated for the recreation of our spirits.

Until we know this in our spirit, there will be no great development of faith, neither will we come into the knowledge of our rights and privileges as sons of God.

There can be no development of the human spirit until it receives Eternal Life, in other words, until it is recreated.

We know this, because there had never been a great inventor, chemist, or scientist in any nation, until that nation received Eternal Life.

This, in itself, is a staggering fact. Thinking men would be mightily moved if they knew this truth.

The Holy Spirit recreates us through the Word. He imparts to us the nature of the Father, and with this impartation comes the new kind of Wisdom. Christ is made unto us Wisdom. This is accomplished when we are recreated.

It is God's wisdom that is imparted to us in His nature, just as His love is imparted to us in His nature.

I have come to believe, as I have studied the subject of the spirit, that when God imparts to us His nature, there comes with it all of the attributes of Himself. They are undeveloped, but they are there lying latent in our human spirits.

There is faith that will link us up with God. There is love that will make us God-like. There is stability that will make us as stable as God; and all the other wonderful attributes that have challenged us in the man Jesus, can be reproduced in us, as we walk in the light with Him.

It is necessary that we grasp the significance of the finished work of Christ; for in His finished work is the recreation of the spirit, and a revelation of the vast possibilities of entering into a fellowship with God, such as man has never yet been conscious of.

Here are some facts connected with this New Creation, some of the new things that come to man through the recreation of his spirit.

2 Cor. 5:21 "Him who knew no sin, God made to become sin; that we might become the righteousness of God in Christ."

It was the Spirit of Christ that was made sin. It is the spirit of man that is righteous with His Righteousness.

This new Righteousness that is imparted to the human spirit gives to the human spirit a sense of freedom and liberty with God that man has not had since the fall.

It takes away from man's spirit the sin consciousness that has held him in slavery through the ages.

Sin consciousness is not of the reasoning faculties. It does not come to us through the five senses. Sin consciousness, or conviction of sin, comes from the human spirit. It comes because the natural human spirit is not in fellowship with God.

The New Birth has recreated this human spirit and imparted to it the Righteousness and nature of God so that it can fellowship with God on terms of absolute equality.

No religion in the world has ever dealt with the human spirit. All religions have been connected with the Senses.

This is something that makes Christianity stand out utterly distinct from other religions.

John 5:24 "He that heareth my word, and believeth him that sent me, has eternal life." This is a new kind of life; it does not come to the reasoning faculties, but only to the human spirit. This life is God's nature.

Romans 5:5 declares that the love of God is shed abroad in our hearts by the Holy Spirit.

The heart is used figuratively for our spirit. This new kind of love, Agapa, is poured into the human spirit by the Holy Spirit. It comes with the New Birth, when one begins to fellowship with the Father.

This new kind of love is not a thing of reason. It is a thing of the spirit consciousness.

1 Cor. 1:30 "But of him are ye in Christ Jesus, who was made unto us wisdom from God, and righteousness and sanctification, and redemption."

Just as He was made Righteousness unto us, just as He was made Redemption unto us, just as He was made Sanctification unto us, He has been made Wisdom unto us.

Just as He was made health and healing to us, so He is made unto us Wisdom.

That wisdom is from God. James tells us if any man lacks wisdom, he is to ask of God. James is writing to the babes in Christ, the undeveloped ones.

Paul, here in his Revelation, is speaking to the full-grown believer, one who has come into his inheritance.

One of the most vital things for us to understand is that we have been made the Righteousness of God in Christ. Not only has Christ been made unto us Righteousness, but we have been made the Righteousness of God in Him.

That Righteousness lets us into the very throne room where we can associate with the Father on terms of fellowship; where we can sit at the table, as it were, and feast on the riches of His grace. Heb. 4:14-16.

It brings us into the place where, instead of asking for wisdom, we recognize that He has been made wisdom unto us. We simply thank Him for the wisdom, and then act, knowing that the wisdom will be there to guide the action.

Wisdom sits at the head of the government. You may have all kinds of knowledge, but if you have no ability to use that knowledge, it is worthless.

You have gathered up the knowledge of His will, of His purpose and plan for you in the Word. After having done that, you thank Him for the ability to use that knowledge.

Jesus told the disciples to tarry in Jerusalem until they received power from on high. That word "power" means ability. They were to receive ability to use the Name with its mighty, supernatural power.

They were to have wisdom or ability to witness of all they had seen, and of the death and Resurrection of the Lord Jesus.

The Spirit came according to the promise, and they received the ability. The world was startled by the incoming of a new force, a new life, into the human consciousness.

The new born Church immediately became a mighty institution in the Jewish country. Then it spread throughout the Roman Empire.

It was the ability of God given to uneducated men to understand something of what happened from the time that Christ died on the cross until He sat down on the throne at the right hand of the Father.

2 Cor. 5:17 "Wherefore if any man is in Christ, he is a new creature: the old things are passed away; behold, they are become new. But all these things are of God, who reconciled us to himself through Christ, and gave unto us the ministry of reconciliation."

Here we get God's new man. He is a new spirit. He is a recreated spirit. His mind is then renewed by this incoming life, as he meditates in the Word.

His body is rejuvenated, healed of its diseases, so that the entire man stands complete before the Father.

The most deeply spiritual men and women I know are people who have given much time to meditation. You cannot develop spiritual wisdom without meditation.

Josh. 1:8 "This book of the law shall not depart out of thy mouth, but thou shalt meditate thereon day and night, that thou mayest observe to do according to all that is written therein: for then thou shalt make thy way prosperous, and then thou shalt have good success." (or, you will be able to deal wisely in the things of life.)

Take time to meditate in the Word. Shut yourself in alone with your own spirit where the clamor of the world is shut out.

If you are ambitious to do something worthwhile, I would sug-

gest that you take ten or fifteen minutes daily for meditation . . .
learn to do it. In other words, begin the development of your
own spirit.

You may develop any gift that you wish to. The most important
gift that God has given to you is the spirit. It is the development
of this spirit that is going to mean more to your life than any
other one thing.

The great majority of men do not think. They live in the realm
of the Senses. The Senses have limitations. Your spirit has practically no limitations.

You can develop spirit life until you dominate circumstances.
Your spirit can come into vital union with Deity, become a
partaker of the divine nature. That spirit, with God's nature
in it, can fellowship on terms of absolute equality with God
Himself.

Do you see your limitless possibilities?

Jesus brings us into contact with spiritual things, not mental
things. Spiritual things are as real as physical things. Your spirit
can come to the point where the things in His Word will become
as real to you, and Jesus will become as real to you as any loved one.

You can see the necessity of your taking time to meditate, to
get quiet with the Lord. You must take time to sit with His Word
and let the Spirit unveil His Word to your spirit.

If you will, you will know Him in reality.

How to Develop the Recreated Spirit

I think that I have found the answer to the problem of how
the recreated human spirit can be developed.

The thirteenth chapter of 1 Corinthians has the answer to it.

The last clause of the 12th chapter of 1 Cor. is also striking
in this connection. He says, "But I show you a more excellent
way," and then he proceeds to tell us the new kind of love way.
This is the love that Jesus brought to the world.

He compares it with linguistic ability, "If I speak with the
tongues of men and of angels, but have not love, I am become
sounding brass or a clanging cymbal."

How greatly we have appreciated linguistic abilities, and yet, with one stroke he has shown us how empty it all is without love.

Next, he tells us, "If I have the gift of prophecy, and know all mysteries and all knowledge; and if I have all faith, so as to remove mountains, but have not love, I am nothing."

Here he is showing us how empty sense knowledge achievements and gifts are without Agapa.

The next verse takes us still further into the picture, "And if I bestow all my goods to feed the poor, and if I give my body to be burned, but have not love, it profiteth me nothing."

These pictures are of natural man in his highest development in comparison with Agapa.

How humble and lowly is this choicest of all gifts. "It suffers long and is kind." It wears the garments of apparent weakness. "It envieth not, it is never proud, it never behaves itself unseemly," (in quarreling and nagging and the divorce court) "love seeketh not its own."

The biggest struggle of natural man is to get something, and he is not so careful how he gets it, or from whom he gets it.

"It is not provoked," it does not lose its temper easily.

"It does not take account of evil, it does not rejoice in unrighteousness, but rejoiceth with the truth."

Notice the seventh verse, "Beareth all things, believeth all things." "Beareth all things," might be translated, "covereth all things." It does not repeat the unseemly things that are said in scandal, but covers them up.

Love acts contrary to every law of the senses.

"Believeth all things," that is, all things of the Father. The Word is acted upon with simplicity and unconscious faith.

"Hopeth all things," you see, believing is now, and hope is future. If we believe all things of the Word, we face the future with quiet rest.

"Endureth all things." What endurance was manifested in the Master! How He endured the scoffing and slandering of those who crucified Him!

But the last sentence thrills one, "Love never faileth."

We cannot depend upon our senses for they may fail us. Our

eyes may be injured, and our sense of sight is gone. Our sense of hearing or feeling may be destroyed. Agapa is not like that, for it springs from the recreated spirit, the "hidden man of the heart."

It is that "hidden man," that unseen man, that has the Divine life.

In Galatians we have the contrast of Agapa and the senses. The fruits of the senses are recorded in Gal. 5:16, and the fruits of the recreated spirit are recorded in the twenty-second and twenty-third verses.

The senses have always been a traitor to the spirit. They are ever seeking their own. They are hungry, and yet they are never satisfied. They are always seeking and never finding that for which they seek.

Solomon said a wise thing in Ecclesiastes when he said, "The eyes are never satisfied nor the ears filled with hearing."

Jesus said, "I am the way, the truth and the life." He was God's love way. He is the only way of life, and the only way to the Father.

He is love's way. He lived it in His earth walk, and He imparted to us His nature so that we might live this love life.

In Eph. 5:1 we are told that as children of love we are to walk the love life way and bear the fruits of love.

Now we can understand how we are to develop our spirits; it is done by walking in love, and meditating in love.

We have come to know that the recreated human spirit is the fountain out of which love and faith, peace and joy, and all of the other beautiful products that belong to the love life, spring.

Faith is not a product of the reasoning faculties, it is a product of the spirit.

Now we can understand this fact, that to develop this recreated spirit, it is necessary that we practice love and walk by faith.

We must feed on the "Bread of Heaven." "For man shall not live by bread alone, but by every word that proceedeth out of the mouth of God."

Jesus put it in a new way, "Except one eat my body and drink my blood." The body was the Word made flesh. We must feed upon the living Word. Blood is life, so we are to drink deeply of the life that He wrought.

He said, "I am come that ye might have life and have it abundantly." It is that abundance of life that makes us over-flow with love.

I have never desired anything more than I have desired to know how to develop the recreated human spirit. I believe I have some suggestions that will teach us how to use wisdom, how to appropriate it in Christ, and how to make it our own, teach us how to walk in love so that our conduct will be Jesus-like.

THE LOVE WALK

If we could learn to walk in love and make it the business of our lives, we would solve many problems of human relationship which we thought were impossible.

Jesus lived in love. He lived in the realm of love. He spoke love. His words were love-filled. His acts and deeds grew out of love. He could not help healing the sick. Love drove Him. He could not help feeding the multitudes. Love compelled Him.

If we could have our spirits developed in love like that, then we could live like the Master; we could maintain a real, beautiful fellowship with the Father, with the Word, and with one another.

John 14:16-17, Jesus promised He would send a comforter, the Holy Spirit. "And I will pray the Father, and he shall give you another Comforter, that he may be with you forever, even the Spirit of truth: whom the world cannot receive; for it beholdeth him not, neither knoweth him: but ye know him; for he abideth with you, and shall be in you."

This "Comforter" whom He calls the "Spirit of truth," or "reality," is to guide us into all truth or reality. He is to take the things of Jesus and the Father and unveil them to us. That is what our hearts are craving.

He is not going to guide us into Sense Knowledge, but into Revelation Knowledge. He is going to take those wonderful truths of the Pauline Revelation and make them a reality to us. In order to do this, it will be necessary that we have quiet hours, a little while each day set apart for meditation.

Joshua 1:8 "This book of the law shall not depart out of thy mouth, but thou shalt meditate thereon day and night, that thou mayest observe to do according to all that is written therein: for then thou shalt make thy way prosperous, and then thou shalt have good success."

That was for Israel under the Law, under the First Covenant.

Under the New Covenant, we are to let the Word of Christ dwell in us richly; we are to abide in the Word and the Word is to abide in us. This will lead us into the prayer life, into prayer conquests.

Phil. 4:6-7 offers another suggestion. "In nothing be anxious; but in everything by prayer and supplication, with thanksgiving, let your requests be made known unto God. And the peace of God, which passeth all understanding, shall guard your hearts and your thoughts in Christ Jesus."

In nothing are we to allow anxiety to govern us; but in everything by prayer and supplication, along with thanksgiving, make our requests known to the Father. Then we leave them there, and He declares that His peace will come (like a garrison of soldiers into a turbulent country) and quiet us.

In the 8th verse, He tells us the things we are to think about. Read it over carefully.

"Finally, brethren, whatsoever things are true, whatsoever things are honorable, whatsoever things are just, whatsoever things are pure, whatsoever things are lovely, whatsoever things are of good report; if there be any virtue, and if there be any praise, think on these things."

We cannot feed on scandal, on nonsense, on stories that are unseemly, and expect to develop in grace. The Spirit will not help us to do that. There must be times when we can sit quietly with the Lord and the Word, and meditate upon it until the Word absorbs us, and we absorb the Word; until the Word is built into our mental processes, as well as our spirit lives, until it absolutely governs our thinking.

Do you see what that implies? The renewing of our minds. The average believer's mind is not renewed.

Romans 12:2 "I beseech you, therefore, brethren, by the mercies of God, to present your bodies a living sacrifice, holy, well pleasing to God which is your spiritual worship. And be not fashioned according to this age: but be ye transformed by the renewing of your mind, that ye may prove what is the good and acceptable and perfect will of God."

How is that transformation going to take place? By the renewing of our minds. How does that come? By meditation in the Word. By practising the Word.

Col. 3:10 "And have put on the new man, that is being renewed unto knowledge after the image of him that created him."

Our minds are renewed after the image of Him that created us. That means the Jesus image is going to be reproduced in us, until after a while it will be no more we that live, but Christ living in us. Or, as Paul gives us in Gal. 4:19, "until Christ be formed in you."

It is possible to build the very Jesus life into us with the Word. The Word never becomes a part of our lives until we act it.

Share your heart life with Him as you would with a lover, a roommate, a husband or wife, until you cry out, "It is no longer I that live, but Christ liveth in me," until the Vine Life becomes consciously your life.

Eph. 3:19-21 "And to know the love of Christ which passeth knowledge, that ye may be filled unto all the fulness of God." God's fulness takes us over, dominates us. His fulness of love, of grace, of wisdom, of healing and ability, has displaced all the weaknesses and failures that exist in our lives.

Jesus has come on the scene to take over our lives. He is able to do "Exceeding abundantly above all that we could ask or think."

He does it according to the ability, His ability, that is at work within us.

THE FAITH WALK

Before the Fall, man had perfect fellowship with God. He lived in the realm of the spirit, but when he committed High Treason, was driven from the presence of God, he became dependent upon his senses for his protection and life.

His spirit became the slave of his senses. However, for many generations you can see the spirit's influence upon the mind. This is seen in the architecture before and after the flood.

They have uncovered five cities built one upon the other in Mesopotamia, and the last one discovered, which was evidently built before the flood, shows the finest type of architecture.

Anthropology proves beyond the shadow of a doubt, that the farther back we go in Babylonia and Egypt, the higher is the state of civilization.

When the senses gained the supremacy, man lost all real knowledge of spiritual things.

Senses absolutely controlled man at the time of the first Covenant with Abraham. Abraham was evidently the only one of his age who had any spiritual discernment. He believed God's Word in the face of the testimony of his senses.

Abraham's faith is the true type of the faith of a believer today.

When Jesus came all men lived in the realm of the senses. If you will read carefully the four Gospels you will notice that they had only Sense Knowledge faith. They believed what they could see, hear and feel. Their spirit had no place in their daily life.

Until the believer recognizes the two kinds of faith he will never be able to enjoy his privileges in Christ.

You remember Thomas as the outstanding exponent of Sense Knowledge faith. After the Resurrection, before he met Jesus, he said to those who had seen the Risen One, "I will not believe until I can put my finger into the wounds in His hands and my hand into His side." John 20:25.

Jesus suddenly appeared to him and said, "Thomas, reach hither thy fingers, and see my hands, and reach hither thy hand and put it into my side, and be not faithless but believing."

Thomas fell at His feet and cried, "My Lord, and My God."

Jesus said, "Because thou hast seen hast thou believed?"

In this marginal rendering that I have given you there are tears mixed with reproof. Can't you hear the pathos in Jesus' voice when He said, "Having seen, hast thou believed?"

Oh, it is so hard for the Sense Knowledge folk to believe! Everywhere they are struggling and praying and crying for faith, but faith does not come that way.

Faith comes by getting acquainted with the Father through the Word. Not in studying the Word alone, but by actually living the Word; doing the Word; practising the Word, and letting the Word live in us.

In John 6 the multitude said, "Show us a sign that we may believe." Jesus said, "This generation seeketh a sign."

That generation did not seek a sign any more than our generation does. Let any man be advertised to speak who has spectacular manifestations, and he will fill the house. Why? Because this generation does not believe the Word, but it does believe in signs and wonders, something that thrills the senses.

On the day of Pentecost a new era began. We call it the Dispensation of the Holy Spirit. That is only half the truth. It is the Dispensation of the recreated human spirit.

The part of man that is recreated is his spirit. The sense-ruled mind is renewed by the Holy Spirit through the Word, so that the renewed mind can have fellowship with the recreated human spirit.

The cultivation of our spirits comes through our giving this spirit right of way in our daily walk.

You remember that Jesus said, quoting from Deuteronomy, "Man shall not live by bread alone, but by every word that proceedeth out from the mouth of God."

God's Word is inspired by the Holy Spirit, and it is the food of the recreated human spirit. As we meditate in the Word, and become doers of the Word, our spirits slowly but surely gain the ascendancy over our sense-ruled mind.

You remember that in the sixth chapter of Romans the Spirit says, "Let not sin therefore reign in your mortal body, that ye should obey the desires thereof." Rom. 6:12-13.

Sin reigns in the senses. There is nothing wrong with the physical body, the wrongness lies in the senses gaining control of our bodies and causing us to do the things we should not do.

Our spirits are brought into subjection to the senses when the members of our bodies (governed by the senses) gain control.

Your conscience is the voice of your human spirit, or the recreated spirit. As the spirit is educated in the Word, the conscience (or voice) becomes more and more authoritative.

I have come to believe that if one fellowships with the Word, under the illumination of the Holy Spirit, that after a bit the human spirit can become a perfect guide. What we have called the "hunch" is simply our spirit speaking to us.

The mind of the spirit is in fellowship with God. The Word is the food and life of the spirit. If we walk in love, the spirit has perfect freedom to guide us.

You understand that faith and love both come from the recreated human spirit. Faith grows as we practise love.

As we practise love the Father becomes more and more real to us. The Word becomes more and more precious. Its hidden assets are revealed to us.

1 Cor. 2:12 declares, "But we received not the spirit of the world (that is the spirit of the natural man) but the spirit which is from God, that we might know the things that are freely given us of God."

Our spirits, that have received their life from God, are able to know the things of God; while the natural minds, dominated by the senses, are unable to know the things that are freely given to us in the Redemptive work of Christ.

The natural man cannot understand the expression "in Christ" or what it means, but the God-taught, recreated spirit grasps it with eager joy.

We can see now that the greatest need of the present day church is the renewing of the minds of the believers, and of the education and development of the recreated spirit.

The average Christian today is carnal, or sense ruled. They are babes in Christ. They walk after the manner of men, or the senses. They have never learned the way of love.

They are full of talk, but they are not doers of the Word. Their wisdom is the wisdom of natural men. They are ever striving, but never arriving.

There is only one way to help these people, and that is to teach them how to take their place in Christ, to become doers of the Word, and not hearers only.

Chapter The Seventh

SUCCESS AND FAILURE IN OUR SPIRITS

E have come to know that spiritual things are as real as material things.

LOVE is as real as the building in which you live, and sometimes more real than material substance.

When we realize the reality of spiritual things, so that we will take account of them, plan on them as we do on material things, life will cease to be excursions in the dark.

COURAGE is a spiritual force. It is born of the spirit. It is not associated in any way with our reasoning faculties.

Reason cannot understand courage which can face defeat and still rise from the mat fighting.

You have heard of the fighting heart, that is a fighting spirit, a conquering spirit, a dominating spirit that cannot be whipped or defeated.

Reason says, "It is all over, you might just as well throw in the sponge." Sense knowledge has given up the fight altogether, but you are just beginning. Your spirit has taken the count again and again, but it keeps on fighting. It cannot be whipped.

I remember in the early days of my life when everything was going dead wrong. Death would have been a sweet escape, but I could not die, and I could not be whipped.

At times I wanted to be whipped, would rather have been than not. If I could have been defeated and floated out with the wreckage that I saw on the stream of life, I would have been glad, but I could not give up.

Somehow or other, it seemed utterly impossible to conceive of being defeated. I must succeed.

My tired brain, my worn-out body cried for rest, but that something inside refused to give way to the desire of the Senses.

That is in every man if he will only cultivate it.

You see, courage is a spiritual reality that rises above circumstances, rises above Sense Knowledge facts, and dominates.

FAITH is another great spiritual force. It is not born of Sense Knowledge. It is nursed in the bosom of the spirit.

It embraces failure and breathes victory into it. It uses the defeat of this morning, and the failures of yesterday, to build a foundation on which the super-structure of Success stands.

Faith is the creative force in the human spirit. Bolstered by wisdom, it cannot fail.

THE WILL TO WIN is a spiritual force. It is the dominating general in the council of your spirit nature.

It rallies the weak and tired body. It drives the exhausted senses in the council of your spirit nature.

It builds sinews into the Senses. It stands invincible in the heart of man; the will to win, the will to conquer.

JOY is a spiritual thing. Joy is not happiness. Happiness belongs to the Senses. You are happy if things are beautiful and satisfactory to the mind and to the body; but joy flourishes, fills the soul with laughter and song when every beautiful thing is destroyed and every pleasing flower has lost its fragrance. Joy fills the whole being with heaven's own music.

HOPE is of the spirit. Hope seems to spring out of the dead embers of a thousand failures, lifts its petals and its beautiful flower into the sunlight.

It is filled with fragrance and laughter.

Hope does not belong to the Senses. Sense Knowledge never produced a single member of the Hope family.

WISDOM is not a product of knowledge, schools, teachers or libraries. Wisdom springs forth in all its beauty from the human spirit.

Wisdom is the cunning artificer, the creator of every beautiful thing, the inventor of every labor-saving device. It has taken the commonplace and made it luxuriant with beauty.

ENDURANCE is that quality that makes certain types of men outstanding in the world's history. They plod on month after month, year after year, with a sturdy self-reliance that thrills.

They bear the burdens of hundreds. Pain and disease may wrack their bodies, but they cannot be conquered.

This is one of God's richest endowments of the spirit.

FAITHFULNESS stands out in the business marts of the world. How we see it in the nurses in our hospitals. But in no other place does it grow so luxuriantly as in the home, in the heart of the wife and mother.

Through all the testings, the trials, the heartaches, the sufferings of life, it reigns a victor; faithfulness, a mighty force that makes the character strong.

NEGATIVE FORCES

We have dealt with the positive forces or qualities of the spirit, but there are other forces detrimental to our spiritual development and growth.

I would not have believed at one time that *hate,* the hideous, monstrous thing, that deformed, unnatural thing, should be a child of the human spirit.

I have long associated the children of the spirit with love, joy, peace, and the many other beautiful flowers which have grown out of that soil. Then I was compelled to acknowledge that hate sprang from the same source.

Hatred, is devastating nations. It is dwarfing beautiful spirits. Men and women who never hated, now are filled with it.

It is poisoning the blood streams of their bodies. It is poisoning everything beautiful in their bodies.

Hate is a devilish thing inspired of hell. It will produce a plague like the flu that followed the first world war.

It should never be given place in anyone's spirit. I would never allow it to gain the ascendancy in my life. It is a poisonous, noxious weed.

Another bitter enemy to which the spirit gives birth is *fear.*

What a deadly enemy to success. It dwarfs our thinking. It devastates faith. It fills the whole life with a spiritual paralysis.

One can conquer it by knowing that he is tied up with God, and that the adversary has no power to rule his life.

Fear is a child of ignorance on the part of a son of God.

If you know what your abilities are, and you know that your enemy has been conquered, as you know that two and two make four, and that two quarters make a half, then you can face the thing that gave birth to fear and laugh in its face.

You are a conqueror, but as long as ignorance holds sway, that ignorance is darkness and you haven't any light in your life to dispel the darkness. Consequently, you are living in the darkness of ignorance and that darkness is a fearful thing.

When you know that the Son has made you free, and the things that you feared have stopped being a destructive force, then you arise and go down life's pathway singing your song of victory.

They cannot fill you with doubt and fear, for you know Him whom you have believed, and you are resting in His grace.

Another hideous, monstrous thing is *unbelief*, doubt. It is a hydra-headed enemy. It often comes in disguise, but the keen spirit-ruled one will recognize it.

Doubt and unbelief are born of the same parentage as fear. Unbelief is a product of ignorance of the Word.

The man who doubts that there is a God is living in the darkness of Sense Knowledge. He does not know the limitations of Sense Knowledge. Consequently, he accepts its verdict without a question, and the verdict is wrong. It is not based upon facts.

When you know the limitations of Sense Knowledge and how deceptive it is at times, it will put you on your guard.

Had Darwin known the limitations of Sense Knowledge, he would never have written the book that has destroyed faith in millions of lives.

Darwin had nothing but Sense evidence. He did not give place to the spirit in his reckoning. He was·only half a man in his mental development. The most vital part of him, his spirit, was covered in absolute darkness.

The way to destroy unbelief is to become acquainted with the great Father God and with Jesus His Son.

This comes to us first, through the Book called the Bible, which is a Revelation from the heart of God to the heart of man.

Another bitter enemy that is born, not of the reason, but of the spirit is *despair*.

It chokes hope, faith, and love out of the heart. It makes destruction seem a pleasure, and a thing to be desired.

It has driven every suicide to his fatal end. It hounds the footsteps of the multitudes who are "hitch-hiking" through life. Despair has whipped them.

I wondered if anyone had the heroism to face despair and conquer it, then I found that one look into the face of Him who met despair and conquered it could conquer it for me.

THE SPIRIT OF JESUS

For a long time I could only see the physical aspects of the Substitutionary Sacrifice of Jesus.

As we see the disciples in the Four Gospels, we see that they only had Sense Knowledge. They saw the Man, they heard His voice, they felt His hands, they witnessed His miracles. Then they saw the arrest, the trial, and the crucifixion. Not one of them saw beyond the veil of the human body that shrouded the struggle of the spirit.

One day I saw that it was not His physical death that dealt with the sin problem, but it was His spiritual death.

His spirit became a partaker of the thing that separated man from God.

I saw that He died twice on the cross. The moment that He was made sin His spirit passed under the dominion of death. Hours later, He died physically.

"Him who knew no sin, God made to become sin; that we might become the righteousness of God in him."

It was His spirit that was made sin. It is our spirits that are made Righteous. It is our spirits that are recreated. It was the spiritual suffering of Jesus that paid the awful price for our sin.

I did not want to accept these things I am telling you, and for a long time I rejected them. I refused to allow my mind to accept these facts, but now I have come to see them. They have become a part of my consciousness.

First, it was the spirit of Jesus that was made sin with our sin. He was stricken, smitten of God, and afflicted with our sin. It was not His body, but His spirit.

Then I saw that it was His spirit that experienced, or "tasted death for every man." It was not a physical thing. It was not a mental thing. It was a spiritual reality.

Then I went farther, and I saw that He suffered in His spirit. It was not the suffering of His mind, or the suffering of His body that paid the penalty of our transgressions; it was the suffering of His spirit. (Read my book, "The Father and His Family.")

His spirit, that had been made sin, was under judgment, suffering what humanity would suffer spiritually.

Then I saw that when He had paid the price, had satisfied the claims of Justice, He was justified in spirit, made alive in spirit, and was made righteous in spirit; that which He had lost on the cross was restored to Him.

He had lost His ability to stand in the Father's presence, and He cried, "My God, my God, why hast thou forsaken me?"

His spirit, which had been made sin, and had suffered the penalty that belonged to the human race, was Justified, made Righteous.

Next, He was made alive in spirit. They could no longer hold Him after He had satisfied the claims of Justice for the human race.

The spirit that had been made sin was recreated. He was made the head of a New Creation, "the first born out of death."

It was a spiritual death and a spiritual birth. It was not physical or mental. This is the reason that the senses (or Sense Knowledge) have declared that the Substitutionary Sacrifice is unreasonable to the senses, but it is the most logical and natural thing to the human spirit.

When He was made alive in spirit, the whole church (in the mind of Justice) was made alive.

When He was recreated, we were recreated in Christ. Phil. 2:10.

Then in that recreation, He meets our adversary, Satan, and conquers him, strips him of his authority, defeats him in open combat, and takes from him the armor of which he had robbed Adam in the Garden.

Then He was raised from the dead. That resurrection is more than physical, psychological, or metaphysical. It is an absolute reality; physically, mentally and spiritually.

He was resurrected, taken out of the realm of death into the realm of life.

It is no wonder that Paul, by the Spirit, tells us in Romans 5:17, "For if, by the trespass of the one, death seized the sovereignty through the one; much more shall they that receive the abundance of grace and of the gift of righteousness reign as kings in the realm of life through Jesus Christ, our Lord." (Weymouth)

That translation throws upon the screen of our spirits the reality of the substitutionary work of the Man of Galilee.

You see, by the same token Isaiah declares, Isaiah 53:4-5, "Surely He hath borne our sicknesses, and carried our diseases; yet we did esteem Him stricken, smitten of God, and afflicted. But He was wounded for our transgressions, He was bruised for our iniquities; the chastisement of our peace was upon Him; and with His stripes we are healed."

It was all spiritual. Then healing of the physical body must be wrought through the spirit.

Spiritually, God laid upon Him the diseases of the human race. Those diseases were not physical; they were spiritual. Just as sin is a spiritual thing, sickness is a spiritual thing manifested in the physical.

Those diseases were laid upon the spirit of the Son of God. He bore them away, and by His stripes we are healed. When He was made well in spirit, we were made well.

When He was made Righteous, we were made Righteous.

When He conquered the adversary, we conquered the adversary in Him. Here lies the secret of absolute success.

Jesus conquered the adversary on our behalf. If He did, then we today are conquerors; because, by His victory over the adversary, we won our victory.

THE FRUIT OF THE SPIRIT

When Paul gives to us his introduction to the great spiritual realities as recorded in 1 Cor. 1:30, he says, "But of him are ye in Christ Jesus, who was made unto us wisdom from God, and righteousness, and sanctification, and redemption."

He puts wisdom first. The same thing holds true in speaking of the gifts of the spirit in 1 Cor. 12:7-8.

"But to each one is given the manifestation of the Spirit to profit withal. For to one is given through the Spirit the word of wisdom; and to another the word of knowledge, according to the same spirit."

Wisdom is placed first here, showing that in the mind of the Father, wisdom holds the foremost place.

Now you can understand clearly the previous statement that it is not a problem of knowledge, but it is a problem of wisdom which knows how to use wisely the knowledge that has been gained.

In Gal. 5:22 we have this great passage, "But the fruit of the spirit is love, joy, peace, longsuffering, kindness, goodness, faithfulness, meekness, self-control; against such there is no law."

This is not the fruit of the Holy Spirit, but the fruit of the recreated spirit.

See the 16th verse, "Walk by the spirit, and ye shall not fulfill the lust of the flesh (or the desires of the senses)."

"For the senses are struggling against your spirit, and your spirit is struggling against your senses, for these are contrary the one to the other, that ye may not do the things that ye would. But if ye are led by the spirit, (your own recreated spirit, not the Holy Spirit) ye are not under law."

Then He shows the works of the Senses. It is a striking fact that we have always thought of these two passages as the work of the Holy Spirit, but they are not.

The first fruitage of this recreated spirit is love.

It goes on down through the list of nine marvelous fruits that the spirit bears in its daily contacts with man. Ahead of all these He has placed wisdom to use knowledge, to use love, and to make love a blessing to the world; wisdom to control joy, and wisdom to witness of the peace of God that passeth all understanding.

It is of the first importance that we recognize that wisdom, and all these other fruits of the recreated life, are the products of our own human spirit.

As we keep in the closest fellowship with the Word, these great realities shine forth in our lives.

Chapter The Eighth

THE CREATIVE ABILITY OF THE
RECREATED SPIRIT

E know that non-Christian people are not creative. We know another fact, creative minds have come from families where there has been Eternal Life.

The natural man can copy and imitate, but he has no ability to create a new thing.

When I learned that creative ability is in the recreated human spirit, I then saw the solution to the human problem.

We know the Jesus kind of love does not come from the natural human heart.

"We know that we have passed out of death into life, because we love the brethren. He that loveth not abideth in death." 1 John 3:14. This is spiritual death.

This is a startling quotation. We know that we have Eternal Life because we love the brethren.

In the next verse we read, "Whosoever hateth his brother is a murderer: and ye know that no murderer hath eternal life abiding in him."

Here is another illuminating statement. This new kind of love springs from the nature of God . . . this God-nature is the thing that recreated us.

Now you can see that just as love springs from the recreated heart, so wisdom comes from the recreated heart. Wisdom is the ability to utilize the forces of nature.

No one will deny the fact that heathen countries have never been able to utilize the chemicals, minerals and gasses or any of the other natural resources with which the earth is filled. Only those who have New Creation ancestry have ability to use these things.

Now you can understand that all creative ability is God's ability. God has imparted this ability to the spirit of man.

71

It is not out of harmony with reason to say that the creative ability evident among Christian nations is God's own nature being manifest.

The vast potentialities of the creative ability of God in us has not yet been developed.

Now notice the statement that Jesus made in John 10:10, "I came that they may have life, and may have it abundantly."

The Greek word for life in this case is *Zoe*. It is God's life and nature.

Now you can understand John 1:4, "In him is life and that life is the light or the wisdom and ability of God in man." (Lit. trans.)

This is really thrilling! In the New Birth we actually tie up with God's ability.

2 Cor. 3:5 carries us a step further, "Not that we are sufficient of ourselves, to account anything as from ourselves; but our sufficiency is from God."

Our ability is from God. God, then, is the bank where our resources are deposited. We use His wisdom and ability.

Now note this statement, "He that followeth me shall not walk in the darkness, but shall have the light of life." John 8:12.

There are two pertinent words in this verse: (1) darkness, that is sense knowledge or Satan-dominated knowledge; (2) light, that is wisdom and ability imparted to us from God.

1 John 1:5 declares, "God is light, and in him is no darkness at all." This tells us we may walk in the light as He is in the light. This means walking in the presence of God's ability.

Jesus said, "He that followeth me shall not walk in darkness, but shall have the light of life." That is the new life, *Zoe*.

What would happen if we should take advantage of that and walk in the light of God's nature, God's ability and God's wisdom?

We would no longer be governed by our five senses. We would walk in the light, not of our sub-conscious mind, but of our recreated human spirit, which has received the nature and life of God.

Prov. 20:27 has this unique statement, "The spirit of man is the lamp of Jehovah."

This recreated spirit of man becomes Jehovah's lamp. He uses it to guide us into the mysteries of the natural world.

What a startling pronouncement that is, "the spirit of man is the lamp of Jehovah."

Man's recreated spirit is the lamp the Father uses to lead men into realms hitherto hidden to them.

Remember Jesus' statement, "I came that they may have life, and have it abundantly." (or as the Authorized Version reads, "more abundantly.")

What did He mean by that? He meant that you may have the Father's nature and have an abundance of it.

Abundance means "an over-croppage." The barns are filled to overflowing. An abundance is more than I can see any way to use.

We have found that Eternal Life is the creative ability in man. Then, if the Father imparts to us an abundance of this creative ability, it would seem as though it would be almost limitless.

There would not be a chemical remaining in the mineral world to discover or to utilize.

We would know how to use what we have wasted and thrown away in the manufacturing world.

We would learn secrets of which we have dreamed, but believed to be inaccessible.

Atomic power is an example of Divine genius. The force was there, but we did not know how to capture or use it. It seemed just outside of human ability, and it was. It was Divine ability that taught us the secret of nuclear energy.

This ability was not found in heathen lands, nor in countries of state-ruled churches. It is only found where men and women have access to the Life that Jesus brought to the world.

Why has it not been given a larger place?

This has been the church's greatest advantage, but she has ignored it altogether.

They have not seen the significance of *Zoe* or *Agapa*.

Then have given *Phileo* a larger place than *Agapa*.

Phileo is natural human love which grows out of selfishness. The desire to possess it gives birth to hatred and murder and every vile deed.

Agapa is the Jesus kind of love, the nature of the Father. It is an unveiling of the Father's very being, and this nature with all of its inherent ability is the reality of Christianity.

In other words, Christianity is the intrusion of the nature of God into man. It is God imparting His nature to our spirits, recreating them.

That marvelous prophecy in Ezek. 36:26 has become a reality, "A new heart also will I give you, and a new spirit will I put within you; and I will take away the stony heart out of your flesh, and I will give you a heart of flesh."

Heart and spirit mean the same thing. Your spirit is your real self.

Now He says, "I will take out the old self and will give you a new self.

"That new self is going to be born of me. I am going to give birth to a new self in you. That new self will be able to know me. It will be able to understand me and enjoy fellowship with me.

"The Holy Spirit will take My creative ability, My melodies, My art and impart it to this new self. Out of this new self will come a stream of artistic ability, of creative ability. It will give birth to a new type of poetry; it will have the very genius of God in it."

This is not a new metaphysics or philosophy. This is reality. This is God breaking into the sense realm.

This is God imparting His own nature to the human spirit.

How little we have appreciated Col. 2:2-3, "That their hearts may be comforted, they being knit together in love, and unto all riches of the full assurance of understanding, that they may know the mystery of God, even Christ, in whom are all the treasures of wisdom and knowledge hidden."

Now we have it: Christ came out from the Father, bringing the secret of a new civilization, made up of a new type of men . . . New Creation men.

When man accepts Christ as Saviour, and confesses Him as Lord, God imparts to him a new nature, making him a new self.

"Wherefore if any man is in Christ, he is a new creation, a new self." 2 Cor. 5:17. Notice the rest of that verse, "the old things are passed away."

The old things that have governed Japan, India, Mongolia, Arabia and Egypt, and all of the other non-Christian nations . . . these old things have passed away.

"All things are now of God."

What things? The New Creation things, the new ability things, the creative energy of God.

All man needs is to have Eternal Life, then give his children an opportunity to develop.

Now you can understand what Jesus meant when He said, "He that followeth me shall not walk in the darkness, but shall have the light of life." Also His statement, "He that believeth on me passes out of death into life."

There are two kinds of death taught in the Word. There is physical death and spiritual death.

"You hath He made alive when you were dead in your trespasses and sins." Physical death is in the realm of the grave. Spiritual death is in the realm of Satan's nature. In Eternal Life, we are made alive from the nature of spiritual death.

"We know that we have passed out of death into life (that means from the death realm into the life realm), because we love the brethren." 1 John 3:13.

Now notice the next verse, "Whosoever hateth his brother is a murderer: and ye know that no murderer hath eternal life abiding in him."

No one has ever known a man or woman, who possessed Eternal Life and was dominated by it, to commit murder. Murder grows out of spiritual death, the nature of Satan; he was a murderer from the beginning.

When this new kind of life comes into the human heart, it is God's nature coming into man.

The outstanding characteristics of this life are love, peace, joy, longsuffering, gentleness, forbearing one another, forgiving one another, holding no grudge against each other.

That is what Eternal Life gives to men and women. They become Jesus-like.

When the Master arose from the dead, one of the first things He wanted to do was to see Peter. He wanted to put His arms around him. Peter had betrayed and denied Him at His trial.

If Judas had been alive, He would have met him.

We are sure He spoke to the men who drove the nails into His hands and feet, and the soldier who pierced His side with the spear, and the men who placed the crown of thorns upon His brow.

He had said those strange words, "Father, forgive them, they know not what they do."

Now He came to them and told them He had died for their sins and could offer them Eternal Life, and sonship, with the wiping out of every sin they had ever committed.

When Stephen was dying, he whispered, "Father, forgive them, they know not what they do."

When they lighted the fagots around the sainted Polycarp, his last words were these, "Father, forgive them, they know not what they do."

How did these saintly men conquer hate with love? God's nature had come into them and taken them over.

Now we can understand the creative ability of God. It is the most magnificent thing the world has ever known. It is the secret of Christianity.

If there could come a new type of evangel, one who would tell men and women the truth about Eternal Life, what it has done and what it will do for humanity, ninety percent of the leaders of this country would swing into line and say, "I want this Eternal Life."

Every college man and woman would say, "I must have Eternal Life so that my children will have the benefit of this creative ability."

The Jews fought Jesus down through the ages because they did not know Him.

The Church has never understood their own Master, or what Eternal Life will do for men and women.

If the Church would present the reality of Eternal Life to the Jewish people, they would stop being Jews and become sons of God.

We have preached the *ethics* of Christianity rather than the *reality* that makes up Christianity.

Now you can understand, "I came that they may have life, and may have it abundantly"; and John 1:4, "In Him was life and that life is the creative ability of God in man." (Lit. trans.)

Philosophy is the problem child of Sense Knowledge. Sense Knowledge gave birth to it when it failed to find reality in life.

Philosophy is purely the product of refined Sense Knowledge.

The philosopher is like the undertaker who covers the casket with flowers to hide the dead. He seeks to cover the dead body of Sense Knowledge failure with beautiful, lovely words. But the flowers cannot give life, they cannot give love, nor reality.

Philosophy has never been anything but the swan song of human failure. It is the blind child of the senses. It has been the blind leader of the blind for the last two thousand years.

It has never found reality. It has never led anyone into reality. Reality was never found by a philosopher.

Reality is found only in the New Creation.

Jesus said, "I am the way, the reality and the life.

Chapter The Ninth

SOME STUDIES IN THE RECREATED SPIRIT

HERE must be a new approach to the study of psychology. The teaching of Professor James of Harvard on the subconscious mind has made profound impression upon the minds of the students in this subject.

Here is a quotation from Professor James, copied from "The Psychology of Orthodoxy," by E. L. House, (page 62.)

"It (the subconscious mind) is the abode of everything that is latent, the reservoir of everything that passes unrecorded or unobserved. It contains, for example, such things as all our momentarily inactive memories, and it harbors the springs of all our obscurely motivated passions, impulses, likes, dislikes, and prejudices; our intentions, hypotheses, fancies, superstitions, persuasions, convictions, and in general all our non-rational operations come from it.

It is the source of our dreams, and apparently they may return to it. In it arise whatever mystical experience we may have, and our automatism, sensory or motor; our life in hypnotic and hypnoidal conditions, if we are subject to such conditions; our delusions, fancies, ideas, and hysterical accidents, if we are hysteric subjects; our supra-normal cognitions, if such there be, and if we are telepathic subjects.

"It is also the fountain head of much that feeds our religion. In persons deep in the religious life, as we have abundantly seen — and this is my conclusion — the door into this region seems unusually wide open; at any rate, experiences making their entrance through that door have had emphatic influence in shaping religious history."

In the above quotation you notice they are unable to locate the subconscious mind, or tell what it is. They give it credit for doing things that only the human spirit can do. But they do not know that man is a spirit.

Dr. House states that the subconscious mind is greater by far than the conscious mind. He tells us the part that it plays in man. He tells us that it is the store house for memory.

He quotes this scripture, "As a man thinketh in his heart, so is he." Here he comes very close to the real truth of the subject.

We know that all the knowledge that has been gained down through the ages has come to us through our five senses (apart from Revelation Knowledge.)

All students are conscious of the limitations of Sense Knowledge. Careful students recognize that there is a spiritual as well as a mental and a physical man. Few have realized that the spirit is the real man.

They do not understand that when God created man He created him in His own image and likeness.

"God is a spirit, and they that worship Him must worship Him in spirit and reality." That is a striking statement, but it fits into the picture perfectly.

Man has a mind that receives all of its impulses from the five senses. The mind has no creative ability. It cannot invent. It can experiment, as in chemistry, but it cannot develop anything that its senses have not already brought to it.

The imagination can only build pictures out of the material the five senses have brought to it.

The natural human mind has no creative element in it.

The thing that first acquainted me with the limitations of Sense Knowledge was the fact that none of the heathen nations have ever needed a patent law or a copyright law.

I knew that the people of India, Japan and China had as fine an intellect as any of the Anglo-Saxon races. I knew that the old Greek minds were on the same plane, if not above the modern natural man.

I knew that the Arabic, and all of the vast armies of peoples in the East, have fine intellects.

Why have they never created anything?

Why were there never any inventors or great scientists among them?

They have produced Metaphysicians and Philosophers, but they have never produced a creative or an inventive personality.

Then I saw this fact, the mechanical Renaissance started after Germany began to receive Eternal Life.

It spread into the Scandinavian Peninsula when they received Eternal Life.

It gripped England, and she began to create and invent following the receiving of Eternal Life.

I noticed another thing, that the countries governed by State Churches, where there are no Non-Conformists, show little creative ability.

For example, Spain, Northern Ireland, Portugal and Italy were far behind England, Germany, and the Scandinavian Peninsula.

This awakened me. Slowly the truth began to dawn upon my consciousness.

There had been no creative ability until Christianity had been introduced.

This Eternal Life did something to the converts.

Did it do something with their mind? No. The mind is not recreated, but is still subjected to the senses.

I then began to study about the recreated human spirit.

As you know, the part of man that receives Eternal Life in the New Birth, is the human spirit. He possesses the same mind he had before he was Born Again.

In Romans 12:1-2 a suggestion is made, "I beseech you therefore brethren, by the mercies of God, to present your bodies a living sacrifice, holy, acceptable to God, which is your spiritual worship."

I asked, "Paul, why do you want the human body presented as a living sacrifice?" The answer was, "Because it is the home of the five senses."

The five senses have been the tutors of the brain. The brain has no way of acquiring knowledge but through these senses. We have discovered that the brain has no creative function or ability. It can grasp the messages of the senses, correlate and classify them. It can arrange this knowledge so that it can and will be utilized to advantage.

WISDOM

The most startling thing that we discovered was that the brain cannot give wisdom. The five senses cannot give wisdom.

We know that wisdom is the ability to use knowledge to advantage. From whence did this ability come?

Then I saw that the recreated human spirit has access to wisdom and certain kinds of ability that the natural human spirit does not have.

I saw that love is a product of the recreated human spirit. It was hard for me to realize that the natural human heart cannot produce a love similar to the love of the recreated human spirit.

I saw that what we call natural human love is born of selfishness. Natural man is governed almost entirely by selfishness. His ambitions are born largely of selfishness.

Then the question arose, "Why is it that the recreated human spirit has a new kind of love?"

The answer was obvious. God recreated the human spirit by imparting His own nature to it. The recreated man has God's nature and ability.

Then I understood 1 Cor. 1:30, "Christ is made unto us wisdom from God."

I saw that the key note of Paul's prayer in Ephesians and Colossians was that we might have wisdom.

I discovered that there are two kinds of wisdom. There is the wisdom that Satan gives to man; it is a cunning, subtle, devilish type of wisdom. We see it in the world today, manifesting itself in lying, deceit, and crooked dealing.

No heathen country has God's wisdom or ability.

Satan is a liar and the father of lies. When he gives to man his ability, it will be a deceptive, dishonest ability.

Only in the recreated human spirit do we find God's wisdom and ability.

WHAT IS SPIRITUALITY?

It is a recreated spirit gaining the ascendancy over the reasoning faculties and ruling the whole man.

The recreated spirit has been made anew with the Love Nature of the Father.

Jesus said, "I am come that ye may have life, and have it abundantly." That Life is the Nature of the Father.

A man is recreated by receiving God's nature into his spirit, which makes him a New Creation and gives him a new self. The old self was selfish, but this new self is Love-ruled.

This new life is like Jesus. It is the substance and nature of Jesus. It is Love's dominion over man. The Holy Spirit comes into the man's body and brings in more Love.

Romans 5:5 "For the love of God is shed abroad in our hearts by the Holy Spirit."

When the Holy Spirit comes in, He brings the Ability of the Father and Son and builds them into us. Their very sufficiency, their strength and wisdom is built into us.

He opens the Word and makes it a living thing to us. He reveals its depths and beauty, its riches and its grace.

He has taken the great Substitutionary fact out of "theology" and made it a living reality in my spirit. My renewed mind is actually feasting on the fruitage of that Finished Work in my own spirit.

The Holy Spirit now is doing the thing that Jesus promised He would do. He is guiding my spirit and my reasoning faculties into the realm of the Reality of the New Creation, and of my union with Christ.

I begin to understand something of the reality of the Finished Work of the Master. My spirit catches gleams of the significance of the fact that He sat down at the right hand of the Majesty on High. He entered into His rest, and I am invited to sit with Him in the place of rest. I am invited to rest in His rest. What a wonderful fellowship this is.

Now I can see what it can mean to have my spirit in such close communion and fellowship with Him, so identified with Him in this Love life, that I lose my consciousness of the past. I live only in the consciousness of my present, my new relationship with Him.

Out of this new and wonderful relationship, faith begins to grow.

Faith is not a product of the reasoning faculties.

Sense Knowledge cannot produce faith, except what is known as Sense Knowledge Faith . . . faith in the things that the eye can see, the ear can hear, or we can feel or taste or smell. That is natural faith. That is the only kind of faith world folks have.

We have the new kind of Faith, the Faith that counts things that are not as though they were, and they come into being. We have the Faith that says, I have what I do not see, but I know that it is mine, and I possess it without seeing it.

This recreated human spirit that fellowships with perfect Love, and with the Author and Finisher of Faith, becomes unconscious of the need of Faith or of having Faith.

Just as Love becomes unconscious of Love, only conscious of the object of its Love, just so this New Creation has breathed into it the quiet confidence of the Creator. He has abandoned himself to Love, and out of Love has sprung his Living Faith.

He begins to act Love, to do Love, and confess Love, and Faith's mighty ability becomes a conscious reality.

Here are a few scriptures that may help us see the realities of this mighty thing . . . this New Creation thing.

2 Cor. 10:3-5 (I want to read a new translation) "For though we walk in the realm of the senses, we do not war according to the senses, (for the weapons of our warfare are not the senses, but are mighty before God to the casting down of strongholds); casting down sense reasoning and every high thing that would exalt itself against the Word of God, and bringing every thought into captivity to the obedience of Christ."

When the recreated spirit takes the throne in us and begins to dictate to the reasoning faculties, then there is a chance for the Word to really gain the ascendancy in us.

When we learn to cast down sense reasoning, that dominates all of those about us, and we stand there squarely by the Word, regardless of criticism, regardless of the attitude of others, then we know that the Word is the Father speaking to us now.

Here is another great Scripture, "Eph. 3:19,20. This Scripture I have given to you several times in this book. I will let Him speak to us again through it. "And to know the love of Christ which passeth knowledge (that is sense knowledge), that ye may be filled unto all the fulness of God."

Really, that means to be filled with the fulness of the Father.

That does stagger sense knowledge reasoning, doesn't it? That the Father would talk about our being filled in our spirits with Himself.

His fulness is made up of Love, the Master's Love; Wisdom, that only a few of us have ever participated in; and of Grace that can put up with the most unruly and ungodly; Strength that makes us omnipotent in our spiritual life.

To be filled with His fulness beggars description! It means to be overwhelmed with God.

You remember in Eph. 5:18 He said, "Be not drunk with wine, wherein is riot, but be drunk (or filled) in your spirit."

He would have us drunk with Himself, just overwhelmed with Himself. To be drunk with Love! To be drunk with Grace and with all the sweet attributes of the Father, Himself!

Well, that is ours. We may be filled with the very fulness, the completeness of the Father.

Do you wonder how it can be done? Let me read you Eph. 3:20, "Now unto him that is able to do exceeding abundantly above all that we could ask or think, according to the ability of God that is at work within us." (Lit. trans.)

The heart almost stops.

Can this be true, that the One who raised Jesus from the dead has come into these bodies of ours and brought into us the Ability that was exercised in that mighty miracle of the resurrection of Jesus?

It is true, He has come in! He has come in with His ability, His wisdom, His love and grace.

You remember I called your attention to Romans 5:5, how He shed abroad in our hearts the Holy Spirit.

The One who brings Love into us has come in and He has brought in that fulness of Love.

He has brought in what is told us in John 1:16, "Of His fulness have we all received, and grace upon grace."

This is ours. We can never be cheap and small again, can we? We will never go back to the beggarly resources of sense knowledge. We will never go back to the shallow teachings of mere men.

How shallow psychology looks now. It is the fruitage of sense knowledge.

The religions of natural men are empty, sounding brass, and clanging cymbals.

We have found reality at last.

The mysticism of sense knowledge once held us enthralled, but one breath from Him has driven the mists away, and we stand in the fulness of His marvelous Grace.

We are New Creations now. We are living in the realm of God.

I know a Scripture that fits into this description of the New Creation, it is Weymouth's translation of Romans 5:17 (3rd edition), "For if, through the transgression of the one individual, Death made use of the one individual to seize the sovereignty, all the more shall those who receive God's overflowing grace and gift of righteousness reign as kings in Life through the one individual, Jesus Christ."

That is not after death, it is NOW.

We reign as kings in this new realm of Life, and we bow to the sovereignty of Love.

Spiritual death has held us in bondage through many years, but at last spiritual death has been swallowed up in Life (Eternal Life, the nature of the Father), and now we take our place in the new realm and reign as the Sons of God.

We reign as kings. We are not common any more. We no longer walk as mere men. We don't act as mere men.

When we go into the Throne Room to present our needs before the Father, we go in as Sons. We have Love's ability to stand in His presence without any sense of inferiority.

His great Grace has made us New Creations, and He has made us out of Himself. God the Father, through the Word, and by the Spirit's power, has recreated us. We are the products of Love. We have Love's ability, we have Love's strength. We can do the work of Love.

From today, I want you who read this book to look upon yourselves and to think of yourselves as the Sons of Love.

Stand in front of the mirror and say to the man or woman you see reflected there, "You are now a New Creation, a partaker of the very nature of the Father. You have received the Father's overflowing Grace, and the gift of Righteousness, and now you reign as a king in this new realm of life."

You have become a Master where once you served as a slave; an overcomer where the forces of the Evil One once dominated.

You are now "in the Beloved." You are as near the heart of the Father as Jesus was in His earth walk.

Chapter The Tenth

NATURAL MAN'S FAITH

ATURAL man does not have the same kind of faith that the Believer enjoys. The natural man believes in the things he can see, hear, taste, smell and feel. (Read my book, "The Two Kinds of Faith.")

It was hard for us to grasp this. For a long time I could not understand the meaning of the word, "believe," in relation to natural man.

Then the Spirit unveiled it to me. "Believe" is an action word, a verb. "Faith" is a noun, the result of action. Then, believing, for the unsaved man, would be to act on what God has spoken.

He says to the unsaved man, "If you will take Jesus Christ as your Saviour and confess Him as your Lord, I will give you Eternal Life."

Then the natural man simply acts on the Word, and the Father gives him Eternal Life. As soon as he has done this, the Father owns him as His child. In the mind of the Father he is a believer and possesses all things.

Eph. 1:3 will illustrate it. "Blessed be the God and Father of our Lord Jesus Christ, who hath blessed us with every spiritual blessing in the heavenlies in Christ."

All things are his, but he may not know it. As he grows in Grace, he will come to know what he is in Christ.

He cannot grow in Grace without the Word. He has the Living Word, the Written Word, and he has the great, mighty Holy Spirit as his teacher so that he may grow in the Word.

As he grows in the Word, he grows in Grace. That is, his spirit begins to take on the Love Nature of Jesus. He becomes gentle and beautiful in his spirit.

He may have been very critical and hard before, but now the very gentleness of the Master has taken possession of him.

The Pauline pictures of full grown faith are a challenge to him, so he feeds upon the Word daily. He studies to show himself approved unto the Father.

He begins to take over the burdens of those who are weaker than he. Romans 15:1 becomes a favorite with him, "Now we that are strong ought to bear the infirmities of the weak, and not to please ourselves."

He has been an abnormally selfish man, but he now becomes an abnormally unselfish man.

You see, this new babe in Christ is growing very rapidly. The very Life of the Father is being reproduced in him. The Word of Christ dwells in him richly. He is passing out of the bondage that held him.

His whole mental life was full of unseemly things. Now his recreated spirit, filled with Love, is gaining control of that unruly mind and imagination. He is bringing it into subjection to the Word.

The Word truly begins to dwell in him richly. He feeds upon it, lives in it. He acts upon it.

The Word has become a love letter from the Father to his heart. It is a daily message from Heaven's Throne Room. It is his communication with the Father and the Master.

After a while the Word abides in him to the extent that his Faith life becomes outstanding.

John 15:7,8 becomes a beautiful reality. "If ye abide in me and my words abide in you, ask whatsoever ye will, and it shall be done unto you. Herein is my Father glorified, that ye bear much fruit; and so shall ye be my disciples."

I hear him say, I want that eighth verse made real in my life, I want to bear much fruit. I want Him to look upon me as a disciple, as a student, as one that is sitting at His feet practicing the Word.

You see, this new man that has been begotten in Him, that new self, has utterly displaced the conduct and the practices of the old self.

People cannot understand this. He no longer blasphemes or cares to go with the old crowd. Whenever he goes with the old crowd, it is as an evangelist. He is out seeking the lost.

He has taken Jesus' place. The Jesus Life now rules him. You know, this is the most wonderful thing about this life.

As a natural man, he didn't understand any of these things; he didn't care about them. Yet his old associates and old life and the habits have all dropped off. He has become an utterly new man.

THE LIMITATIONS OF NATURAL MAN

He is the slave of his senses.

We think of him in the Garden, walking with God as a spirit-ruled being. His spirit then dominated everything.

God could communicate with him with the utmost freedom, but when he fell, his spirit became a partaker of Satan's nature. He lost his contact with God, and when he was driven from the Garden, he became utterly dependent upon his senses to support and protect and care for him.

He is out in a world now where Satan rules. He must have eyes to see the dangers, and ears to hear his enemies. He must have taste to know what to eat. He must have a keen sense of smell so as to detect an enemy or poisoned fruits. He must have a sense of touch.

He lives in the realm of his senses now.

All that man has learned since the fall has come through his senses. Man has had no other means of knowledge. He has been shut away from God.

"Now the natural man understandeth not the things of the Spirit of God; for they are foolishness unto him; and he cannot know them, because they are spiritually revealed." 1 Cor. 2:14.

There can come no spiritual revelation to that man from God. If he gets any spiritual revelation, it will be from the devil.

That is the reason why angels were the agents of communication under the Old Covenant. God could not reveal Himself to natural man, but angels could be seen and heard. Natural man could receive messages from them. A voice could speak out of Sinai that Moses and the elders could hear.

How different was the Pauline Revelation!

No angels came to Paul and told him what to write. God was in his spirit, and the Revelation came through the spirit.

God gave to Paul a Revelation of Jesus, an unveiling of Jesus in his spirit. Then his spirit-ruled mind was able to write what the Holy Spirit had given in regard to Jesus.

Since the Fall of man in the Garden, he has been ruled by his five senses. Satan has been his over-lord.

Natural man had Satan's nature, so it was easy for Satan to reveal his will to him; it is easy for natural man to do the will of Satan.

The Believer has the nature of the Father, so that it is easy for the Father to reveal Himself to His child through the Living Word.

You see, the Satan-ruled man cannot know the things of the Spirit. All that he knows are the things of Satan, the god of this world.

He can understand the deep things of Satan, but he cannot understand the Bible nor its marvelous Revelation.

This Satan-ruled man believes in experiences; either his own, or the experiences of other people. That is the reason that you can draw a great congregation of unsaved men, if you can get some folks who have had marvelous experiences to tell them. This attracts the man of the senses.

SENSE KNOWLEDGE FACTS TO PONDER

We have little appreciated the fact that sense knowledge has had so large a place in the formulating of creeds and doctrines.

If Love had dominated the writers of doctrines and creeds, there would never have been a division in the Body of Christ.

Sense Knowledge springs largely from selfish interests and governs our spirits, holding them in bondage, unless the believer has utterly yielded to the Lordship of the Word, to the Lordship of Love, and to the Lordship of the Man Jesus.

Love binds us together and makes us one.

Doctrines that separate the church were never born of Love.

As I have studied Calvinism, I have seen with amazement that it is but a sense knowledge philosophy that seeks to cover itself with scriptural quotations. Arminianism is the same.

Remember, Truth never separates the Church, never divides it into groups, never makes them antagonistic to each other.

Experiences based upon the senses have caused many dissensions.

In that wonderful movement called the Tongues Movement, immature believers who had received that startling demonstration, felt that they could no longer fellowship with anyone who didn't have the same experience.

Most of us can remember how the Church was divided over the Second Coming of Christ. There was another division on the subject of Divine Healing.

Sense Knowledge was the separator and the divider. Love would have held us all together.

The senses are dangerous teachers.

Experiences, even if based upon works of consecration, of hours of prayer, of confession of sins, cannot be trusted. The Word alone, as unveiled in the Pauline Revelation is the only safe guide.

Don't misunderstand me. You cannot be guided by the teachings of John the Baptist and of Jesus as recorded in the four Gospels in regard to any experience, unless that teaching of the four Gospels is confirmed, explained, elucidated in the Pauline Revelation, or with Peter's and John's unveiling in their Epistles.

In the four Gospels, Jesus is dealing almost exclusively with the Jews, the First Covenant people, who were natural men, spiritually dead.

In the Pauline Revelation, He is dealing almost exclusively with the New Covenant people, the New Creation folks.

Never preach experiences . . . PREACH THE WORD!

The man who preaches experiences and talks of experiences becomes a dangerous leader.

Let Love interpret the Word. Let Love govern every action, every decision of your life.

This Jesus kind of Love, Agapa, is the very Nature of the Father, and if that governs us, we will be governed by the Father.

Remember, that the Word is Love speaking to your heart, not always to your reasoning faculties, but to your heart.

There is no division where Love rules.

Selfishness is always the senses in supremacy. Remember, the senses are always jealous.

May I offer this suggestion. As a child of God, never seek experiences. Nearly all the experiences are in the senses and these experiences do not give faith in the Word. They give faith in Man's word.

They believe in healing because they saw men healed. They believe in speaking in tongues because they heard them.

I believe in healing because the Word teaches it. I believe in speaking in tongues because the Word teaches it, not because someone else has spoken in tongues, or has been healed, or has had some other wonderful experience.

Never give an experience the first place in your life. The Word must have that.

We do not need to seek the Holy Spirit, He has already been given. He is here.

Luke 11:13, "How much more shall your heavenly Father give the Holy Spirit to them that ask Him?"

Notice, "your Heavenly Father"; that is for a believer. That was not written for the Jews, for He was not the Jews' Heavenly Father.

Gal. 3:2 "This only would I learn from you, Received ye the Spirit by the works of the law, or by the message of faith?"

That settles the issue!

But, you say, the disciples waited ten days. Yes, but they didn't know what they were waiting for. They didn't know that Christ had died for their sins according to the Scripture.

They didn't know during those ten days why they were waiting in that Upper Room.

They didn't know anything about His Substitutionary Sacrifice.

None of them believed in His resurrection, even when they saw Him after He arose.

They knew nothing about what the three days and three nights meant to the human race.

They didn't know what Jesus meant when He said they were to tarry and be baptized. They didn't know that baptism meant the New Birth.

They didn't know anything about the indwelling of the Spirit that was to enable them to speak in tongues. They didn't understand it.

1 Cor. 12:13 "For in one Spirit were we all baptized into one body, whether Jews or Greek, whether bond or free; and were all made to drink of one Spirit." That is the New Birth.

Immersion doesn't mean a filling, for when I immerse one in water, I don't fill them with water. When they were immersed by the Holy Spirit in that Upper Room, they weren't filled with the Spirit until after the immersion.

The question we should ask is the question that Paul asked the Ephesians, "Have ye received the Holy Spirit since ye believed?" This is an intelligent question.

When you ask a believer if he has received his baptism, and the believer is instructed in the Word, he will say, "Certainly, I have received Eternal Life. But if you mean, have I received the Holy Spirit, that is another question."

We do not seek for Righteousness. We are made the Righteousness of God in Christ.

We do not seek for power, because we have the Holy Spirit, who raised Jesus from the dead, within us.

We do not seek for faith, because we are believers. We are not doubters, we are the true Sons of God.

We are men who act upon the Father's Word just as Jesus acted on His Father's Word.

This new order of Life, this new type of Christianity that has unveiled to us the truth about sense knowledge and has made us Masters in the Name of Jesus over the forces that have held us in bondage all our lives, has become a Living Reality.

We know now what makes an atheist, an atheist; a modernist, a modernist.

We know the why of metaphysics. We understand why men have become philosophers.

It is all sense knowledge seeking after something to satisfy a hungry human spirit that is craving God.

These people are all in one class. They are all sense knowledge devotees. They tell me they are scientific.

What is science? It is but sense knowledge gathering together certain data. They haven't one thing except what the five senses have contributed.

They are sense knowledge men, ofttimes drunken with the few facts they have collated, gathered, classified.

Philosophy is sense knowledge seeking after God. No philosopher ever found God in the realm of philosophy. It is the child of the senses.

The seeking philosopher finds only himself, for he is seeking in himself. He can't seek outside of himself. The natural man cannot find or know aught but himself. The philosopher is a psychical, mental man.

Psycho-analysis is but discovering oneself. He has not discovered the real self, for he can't find that. The real self is a spirit.

The only self he has discovered is the mental self that has derived all his knowledge from the five senses.

When one searches in his inner self, he only finds what he has already built there or else someone else has built.

Philosophy is a total failure in seeking the solution of the human problem.

Psychologists have called our human spirit, "a sub-conscious mind," for this searcher in his own self-consciousness, has discovered that there is something besides the reasoning faculties.

He can't find it nor diagnose it, so he calls it "a sub-conscious mind."

It is his spirit. That is not the right way of expressing it. It is himself, his spirit, that the reasoning faculties cannot find or understand even if they found it.

When that spirit receives the Nature of God and gains the ascendancy over the reasoning faculties that get their impulses from the senses, then man can study psychology and get to know himself in Reality.

There is room for a new psychology, but it will not be called psychology — it would be Spiritology.

It is knowledge of the activities and operations of the recreated human spirit in its relation to the renewed mind.

Chapter The Eleventh

A STUDY IN FAITH

ONE cannot grow in Righteousness. He may grow in Righteousness Consciousness, but he already is the Righteousness of God in Christ.

One cannot grow in sonship. One may grow in sonship consciousness and learn to enjoy his privileges and rights in the family.

We can grow in Grace. Grace is the first fruits of love. Grace is love bearing fruit.

"I am the vine; ye are the branches." The vine is love, the fruits are grace.

We are the grace of God unveiled. We are sons of God, and as such we grow in fruit bearing.

We increase in usefulness. We can grow in gentleness, in tenderness, in the beauty of the Master. We may grow in love.

Our love at first has little selfish streaks through it. It is marred again and again, but we keep studying the Word, keep fellowshipping with the Master, keep walking in love until by and by love gains the absolute supremacy in our lives, so that we only do love things, say love words.

We are growing in love. We steadily move on up in our growth until we actually believe in love. We believe that love is the solution of every problem in life. We believe that love is better than force, better than going to law, better than the whip, better than argument, better than fighting.

We believe that the love way is the sure way, the success way.

When Jesus said, "I am the way," He meant He was the love way. This new way is the best way. We grow in knowledge of our Father and of our rights, of the finished work of Christ.

Then we take wisdom to use this knowledge. We do not grow in wisdom, for Jesus has been made unto us wisdom.

We grow in the ability to use knowledge wisely.

You cannot grow in Redemption. You may grow in the knowledge of what that Redemption means.

You may grow in fellowship. You may grow in faith. Your fellowship will be measured by your personal sharing with the Master and with one another the riches of His grace.

Faith is a tender plant. It cannot stand the harsh winds of Sense Knowledge. It cannot be crowded out of its seat and out of its place without suffering.

It must be fed continually upon the Word of God and upon our acting on that Word.

Simply reading the Word, meditating on the Word, will not build faith. It will build a capacity for faith, but faith is only built when that Word becomes a part of our daily use, our daily conduct — a part of our daily speech.

As faith grows, Satan's dominion over us wanes. Circumstances are less formidable. Fear is destroyed. As your faith grows, you begin to possess your rights in Christ. You begin to take what belongs to you.

At first, you take the things over that you have merely hoped for before. You have hoped for money, now by faith you have it.

A second thing, you begin to enjoy what you formerly "mentally assented" to.

You have said, "Yes, by His stripes I am healed, but I am sick." You have agreed with the Word, but you have not acted upon it . . . you have merely assented to it. Now you have reached the place where you no longer hope for it, but you look up and say, "Father, I thank Thee that I am what you say I am."

What you have mentally assented to, you now possess.

Believing is possessing. What you assented to for years, you now enjoy. Faith grows in the atmosphere of confession of the Word.

We are not speaking of confession of sin. It is our confession of what we are in Christ, what Christ is in us, and what the Word is in our lips.

The Word in your lips becomes a living thing, just as the Word in Jesus' lips could rule the sea, the winds and the waves (even the fish in the sea), so His Word now in your lips will take the place of Christ on earth.

There is a sick one. The Word in your lips now will take the place of Jesus. If Jesus were here, He would say, "Son, you are healed." You say, "Son, by His stripes you are healed." You are using His Word. That is your confession, that His Word now has become the healer in your lips.

There is another one who is held in bondage by Satan. You remember what He said, "They that believe shall cast out demons." Fearlessly you speak the Word, "Satan, in Jesus' Name leave this person. Go off into the abyss where you belong."

You are quoting the very words of Christ. Your lips become the pulpit of Jesus Christ.

Faith grows with this confession. Faith is no greater than your confession.

Everytime you break the silence caused by fear with an open confession of the integrity of the Word, and you act on the Word, you destroy the very roots of fear and unbelief in your life.

Fear and unbelief grow with confession, the same as faith grows with it. You confess that you are sick, and unbelief grows in you.

If you confess that you have been prayed for and have not received your healing, you are confessing that Satan had made the Word of God ineffective.

And we know, "that nothing is impossible to the Word of God" in our lips. That is a literal translation of Luke 1:37, "No Word from God is void of power."

It makes no difference what the environment is, what the association, the limitations, the mental attitude of folk; here is the Word that liveth and abideth, the Word that cannot be broken, the Word that said, "Let there be" and there was, and the sun, moon and stars leaped into being.

The Word has not lost its ability. Its ability is measured by its Author's ability.

His Word is full of creative ability now. He lives in His Word. His Word has given life to creation; to man, and to the animal and vegetable creation.

"In Him was life (that was the Word) and that life has become the light of men." John 1:4.

You understand that faith, in the sense we are using the Word, is letting the Word of God function through you. It is the Word of God doing business.

Matt. 19:26 "And nothing is impossible to God."

Mark 9:23 "All things are possible to him that believeth."

There has come the union of man with God. God's ability has been linked with man's inability and has swallowed it up. His very weakness is God's opportunity. "When I am weak, then am I strong."

"Nothing shall be impossible unto you." God is speaking in person to you. Just as food rejuvenates the body, so the Word rejuvenates faith in our spirits.

When will we ever learn that He and His Word are one. He is the surety of the New Covenant. He watches over His Word. He lives in His Word. His ability is in His Word.

It is Jesus speaking through your lips when you use the Word.

Let us think of the vine for a moment again. You are the branch, the miracle bearing part of the vine.

You and the vine are one.

You are the miracle part of the body of Christ. The fruit grows on the branches. Love fruit, healing fruit, grow on the branch.

We are sharers with Him and the bearers of His fruit.

Your fruit bearing is the measure of your confession. Your confession determines your faith life, so hold fast to your confession in the face of all opposition. They cannot conquer you. You are the unconquerable one.

Remember that your lips give expression to your faith. Your words are your faith. You say, "I believe; I have." Then you thank Him for it.

You do not need to see or hear or feel. The Word is your evidence.

He says you are, and because He says you are, you are.

WHAT I CONFESS, I POSSESS

It took me a long time to see this truth. After I saw it and thought I understood it, I still could not act upon it.

Christianity is called "the great confession." The law of that confession is that I confess I have a thing before I consciously possess it.

Romans 10:9-10 gives you the law for entering the household of faith. "Because if thou shalt confess with thy mouth Jesus as Lord, and shalt believe in thy heart that God raised him from the dead, thou shalt be saved: for with the heart man believeth unto righteousness; and with the mouth confession is made unto salvation."

You see, with the heart man believes that Jesus is his Righteousness, and with his lips he makes a confession of his salvation.

You notice that confession of the lips comes before God acts upon our spirits and recreates them.

I say, "Jesus died for my sins according to scripture, and I now acknowledge Him as my Lord," and I know that the instant I acknowledge Him as my Lord I have Eternal Life.

I cannot have Eternal Life until I confess that I have it.

I confess that I have salvation before God acts and recreates me.

The same thing is true in regard to healing. I confess that "By His stripes I am healed," and the disease is still in my body.

I say, "Surely He has borne my sicknesses and carried my pains and I have come to appreciate Him as the one who was stricken, smitten of God with my diseases, and now I know that by His stripes I am healed." (Lit. trans.)

I make the confession that "by His stripes I am healed"; the disease and its symptoms may not leave my body at once, but I hold fast to my confession.

I know that what He has said He is able to make good.

I know that I am healed because He said I was healed, and it makes no difference what the symptoms may be in my body. I laugh at them, and in the Name of Jesus I command the author of disease to leave my body.

He is defeated, and I am a victor.

I have learned this law, that when I boldly confess, then, and then only, do I possess.

I make my lips do their work. I give the Word its place. God has spoken, and I side with the Word.

If I side with the disease and the pain, there is no healing for me. But I take sides with the Word, and I repudiate the disease and sickness.

My confession gives me possession.

I want you to note this fact, faith is governed by our confession. If I say I have been prayed for and I am waiting now for God to heal me, I have repudiated my healing.

My confession should be this: the Word declares that I am healed, and I thank the Father for it, and I praise Him for it, because it is a fact.

You remember Phil. 4:6,7 "In nothing be anxious; but in everything by prayer and supplication with thanksgiving let your requests be made known unto God. And the peace of God, which passeth all understanding, shall guard your hearts and your thoughts in Christ Jesus."

Why must prayer be made with thanksgiving? That means that I know the thing is done. I asked for it and now I have it, so I thank the Father for it.

The seventh verse says, "And the peace of God which passeth all understanding will fill my heart."

I am not worrying any longer. I have it. I am not going to *get* the money I need . . . I *have* it. It is just as real as though it were in my pocket. I am not going to *get* my healing . . . I *have* my healing *because I have His Word*, and my heart is filled with rapture.

Your confession solves the problem.

A wrong confession hinders the Spirit's work in your body. A neutral confession is unbelief. It is just as bad as a negative confession.

It is the positive, clear cut confession that wins.

"I know in whom I have believed."

"I know that no word from God is void of power or fulfillment."

"I know that He watches over His word to make it good."

These are the confessions of a victor.

I want you to notice several facts about the relation of confession to faith.

Your confession is your faith. If it be a neutral confession, you have neutral faith. If it is a negative confession, it is unbelief dominating your spirit.

Unbelief grows with a negative confession. A confession of failure puts failure on the throne. If I confess weakness, weakness dominates me. If I confess my sickness, I am held in bondage by it.

These negative confessions are acknowledgments of Satan's dominion over God's tabernacle.

Your spirit always responds to your confession.

Faith is not a product of the reasoning faculties, but of the recreated spirit.

When you were Born Again, you received the nature of the Father God. That nature grows in you with your acting on the Word, and your confession of the Father's perfect dominion in your body, and it causes your spirit to grow in grace and ability.

You remember that your confession is your present attitude toward the Father.

In some special testing that may come to you, your confession is either in the realm of faith or in the realm of unbelief. Your confession either honors the Father or Satan . . . either gives Satan or the Word dominance in your life.

Now you can see the value of holding fast to your confession.

Your confession either makes you a conqueror, or it defeats you. You rise or fall to the level of your confession.

Learn to hold fast to your confession in the hard places.

John 8:36, "If the Son has made you free you are free indeed." The Son has made you free, now stand fast in that liberty.

Gal. 5:1 is of vital importance to every believer. "For freedom did Christ set us free; stand fast therefore."

The time to make your confession is when Satan attacks you. You feel the pain coming in your body. You repudiate it. You command it to leave in the Name of Jesus.

Romans 8:31-37 "If God is for us, who is against us?" Your Father is for you.

Disease cannot conquer you, nor can the author of disease. Circumstances cannot master you, because the Father and Jesus are greater than any circumstances.

You have learned that in whatsoever circumstance or condition you are, to rejoice in your continual victory.

You know that 1 John 4:4 is true. "Ye are of God, my little children, and have overcome them."

Notice who you are. "You are of God." "You are born of God." You are a product of His, and of His own will He brought you forth through the Word.

The rest of the verse reads, "Greater is He that is in you than he that is in the world."

"For it is God who is at work within you, willing and working His own good pleasure."

Phil. 2:13 has been my victory many many times.

Now turn to Romans 8:11, "But if the Spirit of Him that raised up Jesus from the dead dwelleth in you, He that raised up Christ Jesus from the dead shall give life also to your mortal bodies through His Spirit that dwelleth in you."

You must recognize this fact. All is yours by confession, or all is lost by a negative confession. You get God's best by the confession that you have it.

The secret of faith is the secret of confession.

Faith holds the confession that he has the thing he desires before he actually possesses it.

Sense Knowledge faith confesses that he is healed when the pain leaves and the swelling goes down. There is really no faith in that.

Faith declares you are healed while the pain is still racking your body.

Let me state it again, possession comes with confession. Possession stays with continual confession.

You confess that you have it, and you thank the Father for it . . . then realization follows.

Remember, confession with thanksgiving always bring realization.

Confession is the melody of faith.

Confession before realization is foolishness to Sense Knowledge.

Abraham's faith was contrary to sense evidence. He waxed strong, giving glory to God, knowing that what God promised He would make good.

Sense Knowledge has no real faith in the Word.

When the heart and the lips join in joyful confession, faith rises to the flood tide.

Reality of Our Relationship

We never know Redemption facts until we boldly confess them.

We never enjoy our Father's fellowship and support until we confess it.

New Creation Realities never become realities, until we confess them.

Many people who have trusted in physical evidences of the Holy Spirit's indwelling never have any confession of His presence, because they do not confess His indwelling, they only confess His incoming.

They talk boldly about their baptism in the Holy Spirit and the evidences they received at that time, but they do not confess that "greater is He that is in me than he that is in the world."

There is no continual confession on their lips of His present power and ability in them.

I have found that I must continually confess that He is in me. In every address that I give I confess that God is living in me, and that He is ministering through me.

"For it is God who is at work within you, willing and working his own good pleasure."

I plan to continually confess the present day ministry of Christ at the right hand of the Father on my behalf.

Heb. 7:25 is a blessed reality. "Wherefore also he is able to save to the uttermost them that draw near unto God through him, seeing he ever liveth to make intercession for them."

He is our Intercessor. He ever lives to pray for me.

The secret of my success and victory is His continual Intercession. It is my knowledge of His Intercession that gives me courage and victory when everything is apparently against me.

I know that He ever lives to make Intercession for me. I am a victor in the face of apparent defeat.

I know the reality of the love the Father and the Master have for me. "The Father himself loveth you." How that has strengthened me.

John 17:23, "That they may know that thou lovest them even as thou lovest me."

I know His love, I confess it continually. Not only do I know of His love, but I have His wisdom.

I may have all this knowledge, and see the Plan of Redemption clearly, but if I do not have wisdom, I will not know how to utilize this knowledge. Wisdom is love's ability to use knowledge, and so I am rejoicing in 1 Cor. 1:30. "Jesus was made unto me wisdom."

He is now my wisdom. He is the strength of my life. He is the Upholder, Teacher, and Unveiler of the Father's will to my heart.

I know my legal rights as a son. What a thrill went through me when I knew my legal standing and my legal right to use the Name of Jesus in my combat with the forces of darkness.

When I knew my right as a son in the Father's family, and began to act the part of a son, I took my place as a son in the family of God.

What a thrilling moment that was! I was no longer a servant, or a sinner supplicating the Father, begging for this and that. I am a son of God.

Then I learned my authority as a son, and I took my place; bearing my burdens as a son, doing the will of the Father as a son, and took my place as a master of Satan. That was a son's place.

I remember that Jesus said, "'All authority has been given unto me in heaven and on earth; go ye therefore and make disciples (or students) of all nations." Matt. 28:18,19.

Then I knew I had been authorized, deputized to go and carry the Good News. I had been empowered with His might. I had His wisdom, grace and love.

I went out with the confession that I was endued with the ability of God. From then on I began to brag about my Father, and what He did for His children. As I did, the reality of these unseen things began to materialize.

I began telling people what we are in Christ, how we know what we are when we boldly confess it with our lips.

How it thrilled me when He said, "I am the vine and ye are the branches." He was a part of me. I was to take His place in the world, and act as He did.

Then my heart was lifted by this fact — Jesus knew who He was. He knew why He came. He knew what His work was to be. He dared to confess that He came out from the Father. "I have come unto the world, again I leave the world and go unto the Father."

You know, I believe that that was faith talking. I believe that Jesus walked by faith, just as you and I do today. I do not believe that He depended upon sense evidence of any kind.

He knew what the Father had told Him, He knew His will, because He had revealed it to Him. Jesus voluntarily became the Head of the New Creation.

I question if Jesus had any other revelation of the Father. His revelation was not any greater or any clearer than that given to the sons and daughters of God in the Pauline Revelation.

We have the Pauline Revelation, an unveiling of what happened to Jesus on the cross, during the three days and three nights, what happened before He arose from the dead, and what happened when He carried His blood into the Heavenly Holy of Holies and sat down at the right hand of the Majesty on High.

He finished His Redemptive work and sat down as our great High Priest. He is there today making our worship acceptable to the Father. We know that He is our Mediator and Saviour. Not only that, but He is the Surety of this New Covenant.

This New Covenant is not a failure, and whosoever trusts in it will not be put to shame.

He knows that He is now our Lord, seated at the right hand of the Father.

He is our High Priest, Lord, bread provider, protector and caretaker. We cannot fail or be conquered. We are united and tied up with Him. We are what He made us.

We did not save ourselves, He recreated us. He gave us His own nature and life.

We are partakers of the Divine Nature. We are linked up with Him. We are a part of Him, as the branch is a part of the vine.

It is with joy that we confess our Lord and the knowledge of this reality. We no longer hesitate in confession. We know what we are. We are what He made us to be. We know that we are what He says we are.

We know that we have His ability to do what He wants us to do.

We know that His Word cannot fail, for "no word from God is void of ability to make good."

We are just as sure of success and victory as though the enemy was conquered and put in fetters at our feet.

We do not talk about our faith.

When we pray we do not say, "Father I believe your word and know you will keep it." That is unbelief talking.

The man who believes the Word simply thanks the Father for the Word when he prays. He never tells the Father he believes. He does not need to.

Do you remember how Peter said, "Though all fail you I never will," and yet he was the first failure. We do not talk like that.

We know what we are. "Nay in all these things we are more than victors."

Storms will come, but He is in the boat with us, and you will hear His voice say, "Peace, be still."

When your heart is rooted in the Word, when you have studied it and lived it and it abides in you, you will know what to do when the storm comes. If you have been a spiritual hitch-hiker, depending upon the prayers of someone else, you would be in a desperate position if the storm should break upon you. It is vitally important that you "study to show yourself approved unto God, a workman who needs not to be ashamed."

SOME FACTS ABOUT AFFIRMATIONS

An affirmation is a statement of fact, or a supposed fact.

Faith and unbelief are built out of affirmations. The affirmation of a doubt builds unbelief. An affirmation of faith builds strength to believe more.

When you affirm that the Word of God cannot be broken, you affirm that the Word and God are one, that when you trust in the Word you are trusting in God the Father.

You affirm to your own heart that behind the Word is the throne of God, that the integrity of God is interwoven into the pattern of His Word.

Abraham counted that God was able to make good all that He had promised.

God did make good on His promise to Abraham. The amazing thing is that He took a man one hundred years old and renewed his body, making it young again. He took a woman ninety years old and made her young, beautiful, and so attractive that a king fell in love with her.

She gave birth to a beautiful boy after she was ninety years old.

It was not Sarah's faith; it was Abraham's faith that made this woman young.

Doubt was a part of her life. She voiced her unbelief in a statement, and the angel heard her and reprimanded her for it. Gen. 18:12. She retreated in fear from the angel, as unbelief always makes us retreat.

When you constantly affirm that "Jesus is the Surety of the New Covenant" and that every Word from Matthew to Revelation can be utterly depended upon, then that Word in your lips is God speaking.

When you say what God told you to say, then it is as though Jesus were saying it.

When you remember that the Word never grows old, is never weak, never loses its power, but is always the living Word, the life-giving Word, the sustaining Word, the Satan-defeating Word, and you boldly confess it, then it becomes a living thing in your lips.

When you confess that Satan has no ability to break the seal of the blood, and that "by the blood they overcame the adversary and by the Word of their testimony," you gain the ascendancy.

When you openly affirm His Word is what it confesses to be, the Word of God, that His Word is your contact as well as your contract with Him, then the Word becomes a living reality in your daily life.

Your word can become one with God's Word. His Word can become one with your word. His Word abiding in you gives you an authority in Heaven. That is a thrilling fact.

John 15:7 "If ye abide in me, and my words abide in you, ask whatsoever ye will, and it shall be done unto you."

The Words of your lips are the Words that abide in you and dominate you.

This visible Word gives faith in the unseen Word sitting at the right hand of God.

The Word you have in your hand carries you beyond Sense Knowledge, into the very presence of God, and gives you a standing there.

Right and Wrong Affirmations

We are continually affirming something, and that affirmation and the reactions of the affirmation upon our lives are sometimes very disastrous.

You know the effect the words of loved ones have upon you, well, the effect of your own words upon you is just as strong.

You continually say, "Well, I can't do it. I just can't do it. I haven't the strength to do it," and you feel your physical energy and your mental efficiency oozing away and leaving you weak and full of indecision and doubt, and your efficiency is gone.

You see, an affirmation is the expression of our faith: whether we have faith in ourselves, in loved ones, in the Bible or its Author; or whether we have faith in disease, failure and weakness.

Some people are always confessing their faith in diseases, their faith in failure and calamity. You will hear them confessing that their children are disobedient and that their husband or wife is not doing what is right.

They constantly confess failure and doubts. They little realize that that confession robs them of their ability and efficiency.

They little realize that that confession can change the solid, hard road into a boggy, clogged mire, but it is true. The confession of weakness will bind and hold you in captivity.

Talk poverty and you will have plenty of it. Confess your want, your lack of money all of the time, and you will always have a lack.

Your confession is the expression of your faith, and these confessions of lack and of sickness shut the Father God out of your life and let Satan in, giving him the right-of-way.

Confessions of failure give disease and failure dominion over your life. They honor Satan and rob God of His glory.

Here are a few good confessions: "The Lord is my shepherd, I do not want." You say this in the face of the fact that Want has been your master. A new Master has taken over the kingdom and you whisper it softly at first, "The Lord is my shepherd," then you say it a little stronger; you keep repeating it until it dominates you.

When this becomes true in your life, you will never say again, "I want," or "I need," but you will say, "I have."

"He that believeth, hath." Believing is having.

Here you whisper, "My Father is greater than all." What a confession that is! My Father is greater than want, greater than disease, greater than weakness, greater than any enemy that can rise against me.

Then you say with deliberate confidence, "God is the strength of my life, of whom shall I be afraid?"

God is my strength. How much strength have I? God is the measure of it.

There are two types of affirmations that I wish you to notice, First, there is the affirmation with nothing behind it but my own will to make it good. It is based upon a philosophy born of Sense Knowledge. That Sense Knowledge is a product of my own mind. If it be in regard to sin, I deny the existence of it. If it be in regard to sickness, I deny that sickness has any existence. We see this in Christian Science.

If it is a problem of ability to meet a financial obligation, I affirm with all of my might that I have the ability to meet it.

All that I have to make these affirmations good is something that I am, or have, of myself. The Word of God has no place in this affirmation.

I cannot say that greater am I than disease, or greater am I than this demand upon me, consequently, my affirmation becomes a failure.

The second type of affirmation is based upon the Word of God.

The Word says, "If God be for you, who can be against you." I know that He is for me. I know that this disease that was laid upon me has been defeated, that it was actually laid upon Christ, and "by His stripes I am healed."

That affirmation is based upon the Word of God, upon the Word that liveth and abideth and cannot be broken.

Jesus said, "Heaven and earth may pass away, but my Word will never pass away."

You see the vast difference between an affirmation based upon your own will or philosophy and an affirmation backed up by God Himself.

The affirmations based upon Sense Knowledge philosophy have no more value or ability to make good than is in the will and mind of the maker of the affirmation. But the affirmation that is based upon the living Word has God back of it to make it good.

Some Things that are not Faith

"Claiming the promises" is not faith. Faith already has it. "Claiming" proves that one does not have it yet. It is unbelief attempting to act like faith.

As long as one is trying to get it, faith has not yet acted. Faith says, "Thank you Father." Faith has it. Faith has arrived. Faith stops praying and begins to praise.

Notice carefully, Doubt says. "I claim the promises." "I am standing on the promises." This is all the language of doubt.

Unbelief quotes the Word, but does not act upon it. We call this Mental Assent.

I can remember in those early days how we used to "plead the promises and claim them as ours." We did not know that our very language savored of unbelief.

You see, believing is simply acting on the Word. We act on the Word as we would act on the word of a loved one.

We act on the Word because we know that it is true. We do not try to believe it. We do not pray for faith, we simply act upon it.

One said to me the other day, "I am trying to make the Word true." I said, "I do not see why you need to do that, because it has always been true."

People do not know the Word until they begin to practise it and let it live in them. They may have sat under one of the finest teachers or preachers in the country for years, yet it has never become a part of their lives.

Using the Word in your daily life is the secret of faith.

The Word abides in you and enables Him to express Himself through you. You draw on the Vine life for wisdom, love and ability. You are never without resources.

The Word is the Master speaking to you. When you act on the Word, you are acting in unison with Him. You and He are lifting the load together. He is fellowshipping with you, sharing with you. You are sharing His ability and strength.

Now you can understand that all that faith is is acting on the Word.

We are through with Sense Knowledge formulas.

Now we are walking with Him, realizing that His ability has become ours.

Romans 8:1 *"There is therefore now no condemnation to them that are in Christ Jesus."*

Romans 8:33 *"Who shall lay anything to the
charge of God's elect? It is God who justifieth."*

Romans 3:26 *"That he h i m s e l f might be
righteous, and the righteousness of him that has
faith in Jesus."* (Marg. Am. Rev.)

2 Cor. 5:21 *"Him who knew no sin God made
to become sin, that we might become the very
righteousness of God in Him."*

These scriptures have never been majored in our
day.

We have majored sin consciousness. We have
preached the Law. We have kept our people under
condemnation.

Faith cannot grow in that kind of an atmosphere,
consequently almost none of the Believers today
have any active faith in the Word.

Chapter The Twelfth

SIN CONSCIOUSNESS

IN consciousness is Satan's chief hindrance to faith. It is his oldest device. Today it springs from an ignorance of the Substitutionary work of Christ.

The ministers, in attempting to separate the congregation from the worldly influences and build them up in a "Holy Life," have industriously preached sin rather than Righteousness, Redemption and Sonship.

There are almost no sermons preached on Righteousness as defined in the Pauline Revelation, or on Fellowship.

The fact is, that only a few recognize the distinction between Fellowship and Relationship.

Our relationship is born of God. He is the Author of it. Man cannot sever his relationship with the Father, but he may do that which will cause the Father to sever it.

Our relationship is like a legal marriage. The law married the couple, they cannot unmarry themselves. They may do that which will compel the law to separate them.

Let it be fully understood that God is the author of our union with Himself.

Jesus said, "I am the vine and ye are the branches." The branch possesses no ability to separate itself from the vine. That ability is in the hands of the Husbandman.

It is easy for us to break fellowship with the Father. The epistle of John was written to show us the secret of maintaining fellowship with the Father and with one another.

The word "back-slide" does not occur in the New Testament. Why? It describes Israel. The first Covenant people who were the servants of Jehovah would "back-slide" or leave Jehovah for another God.

They did not have Eternal Life. They were not sons, only servants. They had never been recreated. They were servants of the Abrahamic Covenant, and of the Law of that Covenant.

113

We should never use the word "back-slide" in referring to a Christian who has broken fellowship.

We should teach him clearly what fellowship means.

1 John 1:3-4 "That which we have seen and heard declare we unto you also, that ye may have fellowship with us: yea, and our fellowship is with the Father, and with His Son Jesus Christ: and these things we write, that your joy may be made full."

You see, joy is one of the riches of the New Creation. Very few of us have ever made a study of it.

There is a vital contrast between joy and happiness. Happiness comes from our surroundings, environment, health and money. Joy is something that only children of God possess. It is the fruitage of a rich fellowship with the Father, the Word, and with one another.

1 John 1:5 "And this is the message which we have heard from him and announce unto you, that God is light, and in him is no darkness at all."

Notice the next verse, "If we say that we have fellowship with him and walk in the darkness, we lie, and do not the truth."

Remember Col. 1:13-14 "Who delivered us out of the authority of darkness and translated us into the kingdom of the Son of his love."

Darkness is Satan's dominion.

The Law of the New Covenant is given to us in John 13:34-35. "A new commandment I give unto you that you love one another even as I have loved you." The word love there is "Agapa," the new kind of Love.

That commandment is to govern the walk of the believer. If we step out of love by criticizing one of the brethren or saying something we ought not to say, or doing something we ought not to do, we mar our fellowship and go into darkness.

It is amazing how many people are attending Church regularly every Sunday, who know they have been Born Again, but who have had no fellowship with the Father for years.

They are living in spiritual darkness as far as the Word is concerned. They have no feeling for lost souls. They give as a duty, and attend church as a habit.

The joy they once knew in their spiritual life is gone. They are living in spiritual darkness.

Notice 1 John 1:7, "But if we walk in the light, as he is in the light, we have fellowship one with another, and the blood of Jesus his Son cleanseth us from all sin."

God is Light. When I am walking in fellowship, I am walking in the light of the Word, the light of the Spirit.

I am in fellowship with my own spirit. I am in fellowship with the brethren. The blood of Jesus Christ, God's Son, keeps me clean from sins of ignorance which I may have committed. (I have not yet grown up to know that they are sins.)

The next verse says "If we say we have not sinned we deceive ourselves and the truth is not in us." We have lost our fellowship and are walking in darkness.

The next verse clears it up, "If we confess our sins he is faithful and righteous to forgive us our sins, and to cleanse us from all unrighteousness." This is not for the unsaved man, but for the believer.

That means He will restore our fellowship.

Righteousness means the ability to stand in the Father's presence without the sense of guilt, inferiority or condemnation.

You remember Romans 8:1, "There is therefore now no condemnation to them that are in Christ Jesus." There is no sense of guilt for we are enjoying the fulness of His fellowship.

Note this: if we confess our sins, He at once forgives us and restores to us our standing and privileges in Christ. It is wrong for you to condemn yourself after He has forgiven you. You are never to think of it again.

1 John 2:1 "My little children these things write I unto you that ye may not sin. And if any man sin, we have an Advocate with the Father, Jesus Christ the righteous." He is the family Lawyer. He is the Attorney General of the Family of God.

When we break fellowship and ask the Father's forgiveness, our Advocate immediately takes up our case and restores our lost fellowship.

It is vital that we know this.

There is only one basic sin that the believer commits. When that sin is committed, it may throw the door open for a thousand others. That sin is breaking the love law. We are to walk in love.

1 John 4:16 gives us a remarkable exposition of love. "And we know and have believed the love which God hath in our case. God is love; he that lives in love lives in God, and God lives in him."

I like this translation, it has that intimate touch, it brings us into such vital consciousness of our union with Him.

The word "perfect" occurs several times in this Epistle.

In 1 John 4:12, "No man hath beheld God at any time: if we love one another, God abideth in us (we can see God in each other) and His love is perfected in us."

1 John 2:5 "But whoso keepeth his word, in him verily hath the love of God been perfected."

1 John 4:17 "Herein is love made perfect with us, that we may have boldness in the day of judgment."

1 John 4:18 "He that feareth is not made perfect in love."

You may never be perfect in faith or wisdom, but you may be perfect in love. Why? Because His nature has made us what we are. We are New Creations by nature, and that nature is love.

Now we can understand that sin consciousness comes from stepping out of the Love Realm into the realm of darkness, or selfishness . . . out of the Light of Love, into the darkness of Sense Knowledge.

The reason Sin Consciousness has dominion over the believer is because there has been no clear teaching in regard to the New Creation.

"Wherefore if any man is in Christ there is a New Creation, the old things are passed away; behold they have become new. But all things are of God who reconciled us unto himself through Christ."

One of our graphic translators gives it like this, "Wherefore if any man is in Christ, there is a new self."

Man is a spirit, he has a soul or reasoning faculties, and he lives in a body.

Ezek. 36:26 tells us this, "A new heart also will I give you, and a new spirit will I put within you: and I will take away the stony heart out of your flesh and I will give you a heart of flesh."

If He puts a new spirit within you, He puts a new self within you. There is going to be a new kind of love and a new self dominated by this new kind of love.

He is going to take the stony heart out. The stony heart is that natural human spirit that is full of hatred, born of selfishness.

Not only that, but He says, "I will put my spirit within you." He is not only going to make a new self out of me, but He is going to come and make His home in my body. My body will be His temple, His sanctuary.

Col. 3:10 "And have put on the new man, that is being renewed unto knowledge after the image of Him that created him."

Our spirits are called "the hidden man of the heart."

In 2 Cor. 4:16 we are called " the inward man."

In Romans 7:22 we are called the "inward man."

This "new man" has been created in Christ Jesus. He is created in Righteousness, holiness and truth.

This New Man is a New Creation; he is born of God.

The Word has never had its place in our lives. We approach it with mental assent. We lack that steady assurance in this living message from the Father.

I believe that the basic reason for unbelief is the fact that Satan, our former master (whose nature we once had), is a liar. Because of this Satanic nature unregenerate man is a liar by nature. Go anywhere among people who have never had Eternal Life and you will find that they are liars.

The hardest problem that faces our Government is to deal with Nations that have worshipped a lie. They have no truth in them. When they lie, they reflect a part of themselves, for they are liars.

When we came out of Satan's family into God's family, the most difficult habit to give up was that of lying.

We have lied in a thousand ways when truth would have been a great deal easier.

Because the natural man is a liar by nature, if after he becomes a child of God he breaks fellowship, this old sin sometimes takes the reins and rules him.

Lying is so prevalent that it is difficult for us to put confidence in the Word. We have never been able to depend on the words of individuals. We are not in the habit of relying on what others say, therefore it is difficult to rely on what God says.

You see, we have been dominated by Sense Knowledge, and the thing we have called faith has been Sense Knowledge faith.

Faith in the unseen and unknown is a difficult problem, but if we walk in the light, as He is in the light, and our fellowship grows rich and strong, our confidence in the Father becomes as natural and normal as breathing.

We have never been told the difference between the two kinds of truth: Sense Knowledge truth and Relevation truth.

One said to me last night, "If I should confess that I was healed, I would be lying, because the pain is still there in my body."

We must remember the difference between the two kinds of truth. Sense evidence is Sense Knowledge truth.

The pain is still there, but what does the Word say? "By His stripes I am healed." That is Revelation truth, God's truth.

I have learned that no Word from God is void of fulfillment. He watches over His Word to make it good.

Jesus and His Word are one; the Father and His Word are one.

Then I dare say, "In the Name of Jesus I am perfectly healed. The Father laid my diseases and my pains upon Jesus when He was upon the cross. He became sick with my sickness and He put my diseases and sins away, for He was wounded for my transgressions, bruised for my iniquities, the chastisement of my peace was upon Him, and with His stripes I am healed."

In the mind of the Father disease and sin are one. They are spiritual infirmities. Sin manifests itself in my conduct, disease manifests itself in my body.

Before I can be healed of my sickness, I must be convinced in my spirit that God laid that disease on Jesus. If He laid it on Jesus, and I accept that Substitute as mine, then my sins are remitted and I stand before God as though sin had never been. The same laws holds true in regard to diseases. Disease is spiritual, but it has manifested itself in my physical body.

I have accepted the Substitutionary work of Christ on my behalf, so I boldly say (while pain wracks my body), "I am healed," just as the sinner says, "I am saved" when his breath is tinged with his last debauch.

He has accepted Christ and God has accepted him. Now his conduct will come into harmony with his recreated spirit.

I have been made a New Creation. I have been made physically a perfectly well and healthy man. That is a spiritual fact, manifested in my physical body.

The Word is a spiritual fact and is manifested in my conduct and my confession.

Understand this thoroughly: that confession precedes possession. You make your confession before the Father acts in your personal case.

You confess that you are perfectly healed while the disease is making full headway in your body. Your confession starts God's machine in your body.

We have never given confession its place.

You become a slave to your confession. You never grow beyond it. Your faith is held in bondage by your confession.

You grow in grace and power as you confess it.

If you confess weakness, you sink to the level of it.

You should confess that the Substitutionary Sacrifice of Jesus has met every need of your spirit, soul and body.

Sin consciousness loses its dominion over you the moment your confession glorifies the Father.

There is no room for sin consciousness when we know that we are New Creations created in Christ Jesus, and when we know that we are seated together with Him in the Heavenly places, and know the reality of our oneness with the Father and Christ.

John 15:7 illustrates it, "If ye abide in me, and my words abide in you, ask whatsoever ye will, and it shall be done unto you."

He caused you to abide in Christ. We cause the Word to abide in us. It is living and doing the Word. We rely upon the integrity of this Word. We know that no Word from God can be broken. We know that Jesus is the Word. We knew that the Word is backed up by the Throne, the Father and the Master.

We know that the great mighty Spirit who raised Jesus from the dead is dwelling in us, unveiling the Word to our hearts. He is unveiling the reality of the Living Word, and the reality of our relationship and His Indwelling.

He is showing us the reality of our perfect deliverance from disease and weakness.

There should be no sin consciousness in the heart of the believer, for "the blood of Jesus Christ, God's Son, cleansed us from all sin."

We stand complete in His completeness.

"Of His fulness have we all received and grace upon grace."

Chapter The Thirteenth

HOW DOES THE BELIEVER SIN?

THIS has been a bone of contention in the Theological world.

You see, man is a spirit being. He is in the same class with God. He was created in the image and likeness of God. He had to be in order to become a partaker of the Divine Nature.

When he sinned, he became a partaker of Satan's nature, selfishness.

Can you imagine the world free from selfishness?

Can you imagine an eternity with people who have no selfish impulses?

Man was like that before the Fall.

The part of man that is recreated in his spirit. God imparts to our spirit His own nature, Eternal Life.

The law that governs the New Creation man is love. God has shed that love abroad in our hearts. The Holy Spirit imparts to us that love nature so that our spirit becomes the fountain of love just as our senses are the fountain of knowledge.

The ultimate of the New Creation, yes, of Redemption, is fellowship.

Man was created for fellowship with God. God was love-hungry, His heart craved love, so this spirit man came into being. God gave him a physical body so that he could live on the earth.

His body is the home of his spirit and of his five senses.

It is through his senses that his brain receives all of its impulses. The senses give birth to all of the knowledge that natural man has.

Let us look at man from another angle for just a moment.

When man is recreated he comes into relationship with God. With that relationship comes fellowship.

The world is dominated by Satan, and we come into contact with it through our senses.

When man is Born Again, his spirit is recreated, but his mind is still dominated and ruled and receives all of its impulses from the senses.

There is only one law that governs the New Creation, and that is love. We are to love "even as He loved us." For me to break the law means that I step out of the realm of love into the realm of the senses.

Sin, then, is living in the realm of the senses and leaving the realm of love.

When I step out of love, I step into selfishness.

There are only two great forces in the world today; they are love and selfishness.

Every sin that a believer commits begins in selfishness. Selfishness may lead him into a host of different kinds of sin, but there is only one basic sin, and that is selfishness.

Someone has said that the "I, my, me and mine" are the four highways into the realm of broken fellowship.

Sin then, for the believer, is reverting to the practices of the former life. It is a denial of the dominion of love. It is seeking to find satisfaction in the realm of selfishness.

Selfishness causes all of the misery and heartache in our homes.

The cure for broken fellowship is the study of the Word and the practise of the Word, the living of the Word, and the "doing of the Word."

If one is occupied in leading men to Christ, he will not sin.

If he is occupied seeking to build someone up in the faith life, in helping someone, and bearing someone else's burdens, he will not sin.

There is no sin in love. The sin is stepping out of love.
Sin is never attractive when we have a deep rich fellowship with the Father. When fellowship is at floodtide, sin has no seductive power over us.

Sin is breaking fellowship with love, leaving the spirit realm for the sense realm. Sin is letting the desires of the senses rule, letting the senses gain control. When the senses run riot, God is forgotten.

The New Creation man is to practise love and develop his spirit so that it becomes a master over his senses.

I wonder if you have ever thought that a man could become a spiritual athlete, and develop his love and fellowship with the Father until he becomes so strong that Satan and all his hosts cannot touch him.

Those martyrs must have been spiritual athletes as they faced year after year of torture, and still held true to their faith in God.

Eph. 6:10-18, "Finally be strong in the Lord, and in the strength of his might (or power)." That could read, "be strong in His love and in the power of His grace."

Be mighty in the deeds of love. Be a real Samson in the love realm.

You see, the strength of God is love; the wisdom of God is love; and the beauty of God is love.

A strong healthy body is a beautiful body. By the same token, a strong healthy love walk makes a beautiful life.

A literal translation of Eph. 6:10-18 gives us, "Finally, be strong in the Lord, be made powerful, and in the strength of His might put on the whole armour of God (or the whole armour of love) that you may be able to stand against the warring arrows of the devil."

The only shield that the believer needs is love for his Master, and his desire to minister to others.

We can conquer the adversary with our love life.

"For our wrestling is not against flesh and blood but against the powers, against the world-rulers of this darkness, against the spiritual hosts of wickedness in the heavenly places."

If you will notice carefully, everyone of these battalions of the enemy are working against love. They are working against the mighty force that has ever been with us.

"God so loved that He gave . . ."

"For it is love that is at work within us."

"Greater is love that is in you than he that is in the world."

"Wherefore take up the whole armour of love."

Do love deeds, think love thoughts, and then you will be able to stand in the evil day because you are standing in love.

"Stand therefore, having girded your loins with truth, and having put on the breastplate of righteousness."

Righteousness means here the ability to stand in the presence of the Father or of Satan without any fear or sense of inferiority. You can stand in the presence of the Father as a beloved son. You can face the hosts of darkness without any sense of fear. You are the righteousness of God in Him.

"Having shod your feet with the preparation of the gospel of peace." Love is a peace maker.

When it says that the "peace of God which passeth all understanding shall fill your hearts and minds," it means that love has gained such an ascendancy that doubt and fear have been driven out and love has taken the stronghold and is protecting it.

"And taking up the shield of faith wherewith you will be able to quench all the fiery darts of the enemy."

Faith is a child of love. Hatred has no faith. Love is the faith builder and the faith giver. God is love, and God is a faith God.

You are a partaker of the faith nature, of the Faith God. At the New Birth every man is given a measure of faith.

"And take the helmet of salvation, and the sword of the Spirit, which is the Word of God." That is not only the sword of the Holy Spirit which He uses through the lips of faith, but it is also the sword of our recreated spirits.

You see, your recreated spirit is the one that uses the Word, and that Word is always soaked in love so that it is never given in bitterness, but comes pouring out of a heart of love.

You meet the needs of the people around you. You are standing before a large audience . . . there are many unsaved and many out of fellowship, and you are going to open the Word to them now . . . that Word comes from your lips drenched with the love of the Master.

No human being has a shield that can protect them from words burning with love.

The tongues of fire in that upper room . . . that was the flame of love. That was love that had set the Words on fire.

Man cannot resist the Word of love.

The weapons described in Ephesians that we have been studying, are love's weapons for the army of God.

You remember that Jesus told the disciples that they were to tarry until they were endued with power from on High. They were to tarry until they were endued with Love's ability to reach the hearts of selfish men. It was God's ability let loose in them.

Remember that sin is walking in selfishness.

The moment that a believer steps out of love, he breaks fellowship, and steps into darkness and sin.

The believer who sins is one who has stepped out of love.

We have tried to build faith in the Believer by condemning their wrong doings, and by preaching sin and condemnation.

No one ever gets faith that way. Anyone can see that this destroys what little faith one has.

All prayer for faith is nothing but unbelief. Unbelief grows out of a sense of unworthiness.

Now, what shall we do about it?

In the first place one must know clearly what he is in Christ. As a New Creation he has passed from death unto life. He now has Eternal Life, he is a son of God, an heir of God, and a joint-heir with Christ.

This gives him legal grounds for a perfect fellowship with the Father.

This fellowship is based on the fact that this New Creation has become the Righteousness of God in Christ.

There is now no condemnation. He stands complete in Christ.

Chapter The Fourteenth

GOD'S CURE FOR SIN CONSCIOUSNESS

OD planned our Redemption. His Son and the Holy Spirit executed it. This Redemption demonstrated the eternal defeat of Satan. Jesus stripped him of his authority and dominion after He had paid the penalty of man's transgression.

Eph. 1:7 "In whom we have our redemption through his blood, the remission of our trespasses, according to the riches of his grace, which he made to abound toward us (or came bounding toward us) in all wisdom and prudence."

Our Redemption was not a beggarly thing, for it was with the riches of His grace and the abundance of His power.

He unveiled Himself in our Redemption.

It was a legal Redemption. It required Deity to suffer for humanity and pay the penalty of man's transgression.

It was a demonstration of God's wisdom. Man could not have planned it.

It was an unveiling of God's prudence and sagacity, His perfect planning, and of the Trinity's cooperation.

It was a demonstration of love . . . that new kind of love that Jesus unveiled to the world. He revealed His ability to meet man's need and satisfy the claims of Justice on the basis of love.

He was enabled, on legal grounds, to impart to man His own nature.

Redemption was a demonstration of the ability of God to take care of His own creation.

The first thing that He must do after He had redeemed man out of the dominion of the adversary was to recreate man on legal grounds, making him an absolute New Creation.

Forgiving man's sins and leaving him in his natural condition would be of no value.

Man is not only a sinner by practice, but by nature. He is more than just a transgressor, he is an outlaw by nature.

The Father must give him a new nature.

He made it a possibility for us to become partakers of the Divine Nature. 2 Peter 1:4.

Jesus said in John 3:5 (lit. trans.) "Except a man be born from above (that is born of God) he cannot enter the kingdom of God."

James 1:18 "Of His own will He brought us forth."

We are not only born of God, but we are the will of God.

John 1:12-13 "But as many as received him, to them gave he the right to become children of God, even to them that believe on his name."

Notice, He gives to the unregenerate man a legal right to become a child of God. It is not because of God's sufferance or pity; every man has a legal right to Eternal Life.

Romans 4:25 (literal trans.) "Who was delivered up on the account of our trespasses, and was raised again from the dead when we were justified." That is the best translation that I know.

Notice, He was not raised until man was legally justified. Here justification is set to man's account. It is similar to the justification that Abraham had when he was circumcised. This justification gives the sinner a legal right to Eternal Life.

He does not have to plead with God to save him. He can come and meet God and tell Him, "I want to take your Son as my Saviour, and I confess Him as my Lord. I know that He died for my sins, and that He was actually made sin on my behalf that I might become the righteousness of God in Him. I am going to act on my legal right and take Him as my Saviour, and I know that you now give me Eternal Life, and I will become your legal child."

Now notice the thirteenth verse, "Who were born not of blood, nor of the will of the flesh, nor of the will of man, but of God."

Turn back to Ephesians 2:10; here it is stated just a little more clearly. "For we are His workmanship, created in Christ Jesus for good works, which God afore prepared that we should walk in them."

You see, it was of His own will that He brought you forth.

If you will turn to 1 Peter 1:23 you will see that we are begotten again, not of corruptible seed (as natural man is begotten), but we are begotten through the Word of God which liveth and abideth forever.

Just as Jesus was conceived of the Holy Spirit, so we are conceived of the living Word. That Word gives us life and the Spirit gives us birth. That is based upon 1 Peter 1:3, "Blessed be the God and Father of our Lord Jesus Christ, who according to his great mercy begat us again unto a living hope by the resurrection of Jesus Christ from the dead."

You see that the New Birth is based upon legal grounds, and the title deed is the open sepulchre and the seated Christ.

I want you to note this fact: we have been recreated, born of God, and have become partakers of the Divine Nature.

1 John 5:12 "He that hath the Son hath the life; he that hath not the Son of God hath not the life."

Notice the thirteenth verse, "These things have I written unto you, that ye may know that ye have eternal life, even unto you that believe on the name of the Son of God."

We are partakers of His own nature. We are actually born of God. If this is true, then we have become the righteousness of God in Christ.

"Him who knew no sin He made to become sin that we might become the righteousness of God in Him." 2 Cor. 5:21.

Read that over and over again until it soaks into your spirit consciousness.

Say out loud, "There is therefore now no condemnation to me for I am born of God. God is my actual Father, I am His actual child."

Then you whisper to your own heart, Romans 8:31-37, "What then shall we say to these things, if God is for us, who can be against us?"

That is His challenge. He looks upon us as the perfect work of His hands.

Note the next verse, "He that spared not His own Son, but delivered Him up for us all, how shall He not also with Him freely give us all things?"

Notice the two words "with Him." Along with the gift of Eternal Life, all the things that Jesus wrought and did belong to us.

Then hear the next message that comes ringing from the heart of the Father. "Who shall lay anything to the charge of God's elect? It is God who justifieth (or makes righteous), who is he that condemneth?"

There is only one Person in the universe who could condemn, and that is Jesus. He is our Heavenly Attorney. He is the Attorney General, and only He can prefer charges against you.

The devil's charges against you do not amount to anything, for they are the charges of a liar and a murderer, and he has no standing in heaven.

"It is Christ Jesus that died, yea rather, that was raised from the dead, who is at the right hand of God, who also maketh intercession for us."

Notice the next verse, "Who shall separate us from the love of Christ?"

Our Advocate Jesus, our own Risen Lord, the One who died for me, the One in whom I was recreated, the One in whom I have become the righteousness of God, who shall separate me from His love?

Then he enumerated all the things that Satan could do to me, and climaxed it with this, "Nay, in all these things I am more than a conqueror through Him that loved me."

No living creature (and that includes the devil) shall be able to separate you from the love of God which is in Christ Jesus our Lord.

I want you to know that when God undertakes a job, He is able to consummate it. He undertook to set man right with Himself, and He did not trust that work to the angels or to any other being save the Godhead.

He and Jesus and the Holy Spirit, through the living Word, have made man a New Creation, and the very righteousness of God in Christ.

I want you to notice the next step, John 15:5, "I am the vine and ye are the branches."

Here is the utter oneness of the New Creation with its Head. Col. 1:18 tells us that He is the head of the body, the first born from the dead. He is the Head of the New Creation. Out of the Vine, or His body, has come every one of the New Creation folk.

When He prayed, as recorded in John 17, "that we might be one, even as he and the Father are one," notice the language He used. "I in them and thou in me, that they might be perfected into one, that the world may know that thou didst send me and lovest them even as thou lovest me."

Notice the twenty-first verse, "That they may all be one even as thou Father art in me and I in thee, that they also may be in us, that the world may believe that thou didst send me."

The denominations are not one, but the New Creation folk are one.

There is no such thing as man's work uniting the Body of Christ. God alone can do that.

Man has separated the visible church, but he has not been able to separate the invisible church, the Body of Christ.

Some Facts That We Should Know

We know that we have Eternal Life, the nature of the Father. It is not set to our credit, it is imparted to us.

We know that the nature of the Father that has been given to us is Righteousness.

We know that the branch is part of the vine and has the vine life and nature. The branch is like the vine. If the vine is Righteous, the branch is Righteous. The branch is in the vine, and the vine is Christ.

We know that our bodies are the temples of God. "Know ye not that your body is the temple of God?"

We have asked the Holy Spirit Who raised Jesus from the dead to make His home in our bodies, and He has accepted the invitation.

The natural man does not ask for the Holy Spirit, he asks for Eternal Life and to be recreated.

"How much more will your heavenly Father give the Holy Spirit to them that ask Him." Only sons will ask Him, and only to sons does He give the Holy Spirit. Because you are a son, you have a legal right to the Holy Spirit.

In Acts 2:38 Peter said to the Jews as they stood and listened to him, "Repent ye, and be baptized every one of you in the name of Jesus Christ for the remission of your sins and ye shall receive the gift of the Holy Spirit."

The condition of receiving the Holy Spirit was that they be Born Again.

In the eighth chapter of Acts the same thing is brought out. Philip had been down in Samaria preaching the Word. Many had accepted it, and he had baptized them. Peter and John came down and laid their hands on them and they received the Holy Spirit.

In the nineteenth chapter of Acts we have the story of the first converts in Ephesus. Paul found a little group who had been baptized by John the Baptist. They were not Born Again, they had not heard that Christ had died and risen again. All they knew was John's baptism.

Paul preached Jesus to them and they were Born Again and baptized. He then laid his hands upon them and they received the Holy Spirit.

Notice, he did not lay his hands upon them until after they were Born Again.

The Lord has a way of clearing all these things up if we will be attentive to the Word.

Not only have we received Eternal Life and the Holy Spirit, but we have been invited to fellowship with His Son.

1 Cor. 1:9 tells us that we have been called unto fellowship with Jesus Christ. That ties up with 2 Cor. 6:1, "And working together with Him."

You see, we are laborers together with Him. Fellowship means that I have assumed the burdens of the Master. I am His fellow-helper. I am laboring together with Him.

The branch is the fruit-bearing part of Christ. The fruit I bear is not only my spiritual development and growth in grace, but it is the souls I gain and the believers that I lead into their inheritance and rights and privileges in Christ.

I have become an heir of God and a joint heir with Christ that I may bring forth fruit.

The man who does not bring forth fruit will eventually lose his fellowship.

Sonship, righteousness, and the Indwelling One will bring no joy to his heart, because he has failed to be a fruit-bearing branch.

Chapter The Fifteenth

A JOYFUL CONFESSION

ETERNAL Life gives to the Believer an unknown element the world had never before had. It is a thing that Peter called, "Joy unspeakable and full of glory."

We understand that happiness comes from environment, but joy comes from within and is a product of the New Creation.

We found that the martyrs had joy unspeakable even when dying in physical agony. That stirred the multitudes that thronged about, but it startled the thinking portion of the crowds. How could they be so full of joy when they knew that death was near?

Others have witnessed joy in the midst of deepest sorrow.

It is an unquenchable something.

Evangelists have discovered that joy is the secret of real evangelism. The joyful Christians are a good advertisement.

John 15:11, Jesus says these strange words, "These things have I spoken unto you, that my joy may be in you, and that your joy may be made full."

In giving the great charter promise in regard to the use of His Name, Jesus said, "Hitherto have ye asked nothing in my name: ask and ye shall receive, that your joy may be made full." John 16:24.

In John 17:13 Jesus speaks these words, "Now I come to thee; and these things speak I in the world, that they may have my joy made full in themselves."

This is the very climax of this divine life.

That is a thought-arresting sentence . . . "that your joy may be made full."

We are going to find something in the Name of Jesus that will give us joy in a measure that we have never before known.

I know the thrill that came to me when I saw one of my teachers at Bethel, years ago, come back from the jaws of death because of the power in that Name.

I saw a dead arm that had been useless for years become perfectly well and normal instantly in that almighty Name.

When I saw broken bones instantly made whole, strange joy, an unspeakable thing, filled me.

When Brother Fredericks of Seattle was healed, his dead paralyzed hands instantly became normal. The body that was ninety-five percent dead (according to the authorities at the hospital) became a new body. The cancer of the colon stopped being. The neuralgia of the heart stopped. The stomach that could not digest food was instantly perfect. The legs that were almost useless became strong and normal in a moment.

It was the power and authority enwrapped in that Name.

I have seen people with arthritis perfectly delivered in that Name.

I have noticed in Evangelistic meetings that it is the joyful, living testimony that stirs the people.

It is the person who is so full of joy that he can hardly speak, as the tears stream down his face, that moves the people.

In other words, it is the joyful confession that touches hearts.

The reluctant, hesitant confession shows that the one who is speaking is not certain that the Word will make good, or has made good.

Faith's Confession

Faith's confession is always a joyful confession. It confesses that we have the money before it has arrived. It confesses perfect healing while the pain is still in the body. It confesses victory while defeat still holds it captive.

Your confession is based upon the living Word. "I know whom I have believed and I am persuaded that He is not only able to make good, but He is making good now in my case."

I prayed for one who was very ill. After I had finished praying, the person said, "I know I am going to get well."

I knew that we were defeated, and I said to her, "When are you going to get well?"

She said, "I do not know when, but I know I will, for the Word cannot fail me."

I said, "No, but you have failed the Word. The Word is NOW, faith is NOW. Is the Word true in your case?"

She said, "Yes, indeed it is true."

"Then," I said, "by His stripes, what?"

She saw it. "Why, by His stripes I *am* healed."

I said, "When?" She said, "Now."

I said, "You had better get up and dress, then."

I remember an aged man in Fredericton, New Brunswick, a deacon in the Baptist Church there, who came down with double pneumonia. Several of the local pastors and I went up to pray for him. I anointed him and we prayed. After we prayed he said with a strong voice, "Wife, get my clothes, I am getting up." That was joy acting on the Word.

When we confess the Word with joy, it brings conviction to the listeners.

In Romans 10:10 it says, "For with the heart man believeth." I like to translate it like this, "For with the heart, man acts on the Word."

The heart acts and that drives the lips to confession.

A doubting heart is a sense-ruled heart.

A fearless confession comes from a Word-ruled heart. The Word dominates their heart life and they speak as did Paul, "I know in whom I have believed."

As Paul stood on the deck of that ship in the midst of the awful storm, he said, "I believe God." Then he told those wondering men, "Every one of you will get to the shore safely, but the ship will be lost."

He said, "Come, let us eat breakfast." He broke bread and gave thanks in the midst of them. He gave them more than bread, he gave them courage.

Paul had a faith-filled, joyous confession.

Only a heart that is nourished on the Word can stand in these hard places.

When we know that the Word is God speaking to us now, it is not difficult to act upon it.

In the Eighty-second Psalm it declares that "the Word is settled in heaven." When I read that, I saw that it must be settled in my heart. I would no longer "try" to settle it. I knew that no Word from God was void of fulfillment. I was no longer afraid to act upon it.

The Word became more real to me than any word man had ever spoken. My lips were filled with laughter, my heart was filled with joy, and I had a victorious confession.

How many times have I seen the hesitant confession a forerunner of failure, and the joyful confession a forerunner of victory.

When we fearlessly act upon the Word and joyfully cast our every care on Him, victory is as sure as the rising of the sun.

Chapter The Sixteenth

RELATION OF CONFESSION TO WISDOM AND SUCCESS

NE does not enjoy more of the reality of spiritual truth than he confesses. Man's faith is measured by his confession. His joy is measured by his confession.

We receive wisdom only in the measure that we confess that Christ is our wisdom.

We should make this confession continually.

"I thank thee, Father, that thou didst make Jesus wisdom unto me. So I know that today as I walk in fellowship with the Word, His wisdom will be mine at every crisis."

This continual confession of Christ as your wisdom will transform your entire conduct. You will find that your conversation will take on a loftier aspect; your thinking will swing out of the old groove that your inferiority complex has given you, into a new realm of positive action. There will be the consciousness of co-operation with Him.

This is not psychology or metaphysics. This is absolute fact.

God becomes a part of our very consciousness.

This continual confession will eventually give our spirit control of our reasoning faculties.

We must continually reiterate this truth, for wisdom is not of the intellect. It cannot be imparted to us by man. This kind of wisdom comes down from above, and comes in response to our acting on the Word.

It will be well to pause a moment in our activities and let Him take us over in our spirit consciousness.

God only responds to us as we act upon His Word.

The electricity is in your room. It is wired, everything is in perfect condition. All you need to do is to touch the button.

So it is in this divine life. The ability of God is at your disposal. It is there with you. The fact is, in a very large measure it is in you, but it lies dormant until you act upon the Word.

In other words, until you place your utter dependence in Him and expect Him to cooperate with you, God's ability lies dormant in you.

There must grow in you the sense of His presence in you, learning to depend on Him, and expecting Him to respond to you moment by moment as you need Him. This will develop in you a spiritual sensitiveness to His spirit. You will discover His ability gaining the ascendancy over your faculties, until after a while you will live in the realm of the superman.

WHAT WE NEED TO PUT US OVER

I am conscious that you who are reading this book are hungry for success, whether it be in the financial, political, social or spiritual realm. You are not content with yourself as you are.

My part in the drama is to awaken in you the hidden forces that you already possess, and begin to draw them out.

You remember that the word "educate" means "to draw out." We have thought that it meant to cram and load our minds with facts. That is not education. That is accumulation of knowledge that may be of no value whatever.

I remember when 80% of the theological course was non-usable knowledge in actual ministry. That showed a lack of wisdom on the part of the instructors. It should have been 80% usable knowledge and 20% non-usable.

It is a known fact that 80% of the knowledge that is accumulated in schools, colleges, reading and observation, is not used by the average person. We are not using more than 10% of our abilities and knowledge.

Here is a man who knows it is not good to smoke, but he smokes just the same. He knows it is not good for his body to stay up half the night carousing and dancing. He knows that he is not living up to his knowledge. He knows he should not make a glutton of himself, he should not eat certain things and drink certain things. He is not using his knowledge. He lacks wisdom.

If that man were wise, he would cut out the drinking and smoking at once.

If that woman were wise, she would not smoke another cigarette.

You know you should spend more time in study. You know you should stop wasting your time in foolish conversation and talk, and begin to utilize the forces in you and the opportunities that you can make for study and mental improvement.

You know that you could have an increase in salary where you work if you applied yourself, but you are living to gratify your senses. The thing you need is wisdom.

Wisdom is crying at the gate; her voice is heard at the portal of every business house, and men are heedless of her warning. They are not using the gifts that God has given to them. They are not acting on the knowledge that will make them successful and happy.

Wisdom's cry is ignored.

Do you want to go over the top? Are you unsatisfied with your salary? All right, then, let us take inventory. What have you in you that is worthwhile?

Two things are necessary: first, find the gift; second, drive yourself to develop that gift until it is of commercial value.

Maybe you have a good voice, but it is of no value to you. If it were developed and trained, it would bring a splendid income. You are saying, "I have a good voice, I have natural ability."

It has a thrill in it when you are about eighteen or twenty years of age, but if that gift is not developed when you are thirty, you are ashamed, and you take the position that your inferiority complex is forcing upon you. You are getting the spirit of a conquered, whipped person, rather than that of a dominant one.

Perhaps you have some other ability. It lies there dormant like gold in the stream where a thousand boats have passed over it, and thousands of men and women have bathed in the waters. Beneath their feet was a fortune, but they did not know it.

You have seen all this ability in yourself; you have played with it as carelessly as those swimmers, or as those men and women who are riding over that gold.

Wisdom is crying today. She has made her feast; she is inviting you to come and join her, but you persist in rejecting her solicitations and ignoring her warnings.

I wonder if you ever read the first chapter of Proverbs?

"Wisdom crieth aloud in the street; she uttereth her voice in the broad places; she crieth in the chief place of concourse; at the entrance of the gates, in the city, she uttereth her words: How long, ye simple ones, will ye love simplicity? And scoffers delight them in scoffing, and fools hate knowledge? Turn you at my reproof: Behold, I will pour out my spirit upon you; I will make known my words unto you. Because I have called, and ye have refused; I have stretched out my hand, and no man hath regarded; but ye have set at nought all my counsel, and would none of my reproof: I also will laugh in the day of your calamity; I will mock when your fear cometh; when your fear cometh as a storm, and your calamity cometh on as a whirlwind: when distress and anguish come upon you. Then will you seek for me, but you cannot find me. You will search for me and cry loudly, but I will not be there."

Why? You hated wisdom. You would not let God give to you what belonged to you.

All over the land, men and women are suffering the penalty of turning down wisdom. Every city has its rendezvous of broken lives, of wrecked manhood and womanhood. Every large city has its "skid road." Go down there any warm night and see the streets literally jammed with men and women. Every one of them are failures. The majority show by their faces that they had talent and ability. Many of them are college men. What is the trouble? It is lack of wisdom.

Yet, wisdom is available to every man. No man needs to be a failure.

Here are some facts on which you can base your legal rights to wisdom.

I am going to prove to you that the ability of God is at your disposal, that the mind of God can be absorbed by your mind, the will of God can be incorporated into your will, and the health and vigor of God can become a part of your body, so you will have the strength of God, the ability of God, and the wisdom of God.

If this is not a challenge, then what can challenge the ambitious?

You may have His wisdom in your daily life. Not only is that a promise, but it is an absolute certainty. You may have cooperation with the source of all wisdom.

It is a wonderful thing to have a lawyer on whom you can call for his opinion in doubtful problems, but here is something infinitely beyond any lawyer that money can employ. Here is the ability of God at your disposal.

Col. 1:12 (notice this translation), "Giving thanks unto the Father who has given us the ability to enjoy our share of the inheritance of the saints in light."

He has given to you the ability. It is in you. When you were Born Again, you received His nature, His substance, His life, and along with that New Birth was offered to you the Holy Spirit to be continually in your body.

When Jesus promised that the Holy Spirit would come and lead us into all truth, He meant exactly what He said.

God's ability is freely offered to every one of us.

Note these facts, "Who delivered us out of the authority of darkness and translated us into the kingdom of the Son of his love; in whom we have our redemption, the remission of our sins."

He has delivered us out of the authority of darkness.

Turn back to 2 Cor. 4:4 and see the condition of the average mind: "If our good news is veiled, it is veiled in them that are perishing, in whom the God of this age has blinded the minds of the unbelieving."

That is a serious thing. The minds of the unbelieving are blinded.

Romans 1:28 "And even as they refused to have God in their knowledge, God gave them up unto a reprobate mind, to do those things which are not fitting."

They refused to have God's knowledge, God's wisdom and ability, so He withdrew and left them alone.

Satan came in and filled their minds with darkness.

Look at the heathen nations; look at the nations that are without God; look at the nations devastated by war. Do you see the darkness of the human mind?

Eph. 4:17 "This I say, therefore, and testify in the Lord, that ye no longer walk as the Gentiles also walk, in the vanity of their mind, being darkened in their understanding, alienated from the life of God, because of the ignorance that is in them, because of the hardening of their heart."

This is the natural mind that God has redeemed out of this darkness, yet so few take advantage of this Redemption.

2 Cor. 5:17 "Wherefore if any man is in Christ, he is a new creature: the old things are passed away; behold, they are become new. But all things are of God, who reconciled us to himself through Christ, and gave unto us the ministry of reconciliation."

This darkened mind, this mind held in subjection by ignorance, now comes in contact with God. The spirit is recreated, receives the nature and life of God, and the mind now becomes renewed in knowledge after the image of Him that created him.

The moment that the spirit is recreated, the mind may be renewed and brought into perfect harmony with the recreated spirit by the study of the Word. It may take a little time, but it is worth the effort.

When this mind is renewed and brought into fellowship with the recreated spirit, then we are able to receive the wisdom from God.

Wisdom is in the Word of God. The Spirit will illuminate the scripture and you will understand the mind of the Father.

I have been amazed in my own searching after these mighty truths, to see how real they become to the human consciousness.

The basic law of wisdom is found in love. Wisdom never acts out of love. Wisdom always follows after love. God is all wise, but God is love. All of God's activities are in the realm of love. God never acts outside of Love. If justice is demanded, it is demanded by love.

When this mighty truth really gains the ascendancy, then this new kind of love will dominate your thinking and conduct. You understand, it is the nature of the Father manifesting itself in the lives of His children.

The man who walks in this new kind of love never makes a mistake, never does wrong. There is no sin in love. There is sin in the old love, the natural love of the human heart, but in the love of the recreated spirit there is no sin.

There is no law in the realm of love except love itself. It makes its own law. Its law is above the law of the Senses.

To walk in love is to walk in God, and to walk in God is to walk in wisdom, and to walk in wisdom is success. Then you will have arrived at the highest order of spiritual perception. You will walk in the realm of success; you will walk where Jesus would have walked were He in your place.

You cannot conceive of Jesus being a failure, of a Jesus man or woman with a Jesus-directed mind being a failure.

Success grows out of wisdom, and wisdom grows out of love.

THE RELATION OF ETERNAL LIFE TO WISDOM AND SUCCESS

One of the most significant sentences uttered by the Master is found in John 10:10. "I came that they may have life, and may have it abundantly."

Our theological friends have ignored this, but this is the objective of Christ's coming. This is the reason for the Incarnation, the reason for Calvary and the suffering of the Man of Galilee.

"I came that they may have life."

"He that believeth on me hath passed out of death into life."

"He that believeth on me hath Eternal Life and cometh not into judgment, but has passed out of the realm of Satan into the realm of God." (lit. trans.)

That is an amazing thing!

What is this Eternal Life, and what effect will it have upon us when we receive it?

Here are the facts: No nation has ever needed a copyright or a patent law until this Eternal Life came to them. When this Eternal Life comes into a man's spirit, especially a young man, it increases his ability and efficiency from ten to one hundred percent.

Can you imagine what it would mean to have your spirit not only dominated by this life, but made alive with this life, filled with this life?

Just as the tree is made alive with the sap that comes to it from the ground through the roots, so your spirit would be made alive with the new life pouring in from God's heart.

Can you see how that would revolutionize lives?

I am convinced that not one percent of the down and out, men who are continually out of employment, have ever received Eternal Life.

I question if you can find one percent of the boys and girls who are in the reformatories that have ever received Eternal Life. If they had received Eternal Life, they would not be there.

Eternal Life is the nature of God, and it absolutely destroys the pleasure that one would find in criminality. There is no pleasure for the man or woman to live in sin after they have received Eternal Life.

Did you ever notice or consider the fact that following every real spiritual awakening, where multitudes of young men and women are Born Again, that there is an exodus to schools and colleges.

Just as soon as a man receives Eternal Life, he wants an education.

At the time I was Born Again, I was working in a factory. I had no education whatever. The third night when I came home from the service my mother asked me where I had been, and I told her.

My brother, older than I, a witty fellow, said, "Mother, that fool will be preaching next."

I ran upstairs to get away from him, for I dreaded his wit, but I said as I went, "Eddie, you are right; I am going to have an education, and I am going to preach."

Eternal Life had come into my spirit and my old life dropped away from me. At once I became a student.

Eternal Life promises wisdom.

John, writing, said, "These things have I written unto you that ye may know that ye have Eternal Life, even to you that believe on the name."

The Christian can bank on Eternal Life just as you can reckon on the money you have down in the bank.

Now I say to myself, "I have the nature of God in me. I cannot be conquered. I cannot be whipped. No matter what the appearances may be, I am a victor, I am an overcomer. The world's forces may dominate for the time being, but I am bound to come out on top. Why? Because "greater is He that is in me than he that is in the world."

Who is that "He" that is in me? It is God. It is the great Holy Spirit that Jesus promised before He went away. He said, "Ye shall receive power after that the Holy Spirit is come upon you; and I want you to tarry in Jerusalem until He comes."

The word "power" comes from the Greek word "dunamis" which means ability. Ability means wisdom.

He said, "I want you to tarry in Jerusalem until the ability of God, the wisdom of God, has come to you."

The thing that characterized the speakers of the early church was their profound wisdom. They were able to meet the fearful opposition and the dangerous crises that seemed to confront them daily, and win.

They were more than masters over all their enemies. They dominated Jerusalem, and soon dominated the whole Roman Empire. The ability of God had come to them.

Now He said, "How much more will your Heavenly Father give the Holy Spirit to them that ask Him."

He is talking to His sons and daughters. You have access to the ability of God, to the wisdom of God. You are not left stranded, not knowing which way to go.

You are starting out today with the Guide living in you. You would get lost if you tried to walk alone, and I know that you would fail.

When men try to scale a lofty mountain, they have a guide. You are climbing something more dangerous than the Alps or Mount Everest, and you need a guide.

"When He, the Spirit of truth is come, He will guide you into all the truth."

This Spirit-Guide is offering His services to every one of us. They are free. They are love given.

Can't you see that the source of wisdom lies in this mighty personality who comes into your life?

Can't you see that if you are tied up with God, you at once become a superman.

Our Christian leaders have told us that we must be humble and self-effacing, and always talking about our weaknesses, but what does the Word tell us? God says, "Ye are of God, and have overcome them." There is no inferiority complex in that!

"Nay in all these things we are more than conquerors."

"Giving thanks unto the Father who always leadeth us in triumph."

Does that harmonize with the false teachings of an assumed humility? Not a bit of it! That is the voice of a victor . . . the voice of triumph.

You have God's nature, God's ability. You are God's child. God is the strength of your life. He is made unto us Wisdom, Sanctification, Redemption and Righteousness. If He was made this unto us, this is what we are.

He was made sin, who knew no sin, that you, who knew no Righteousness, might be made the Righteousness of God in Him.

We are His workmanship, created in Christ Jesus.

We are the triumphant, victorious ones. This is ours. This mighty thing is ours!

You are not a slave, you are a free man.

This New Testament is the "Good News" of our emancipation, and of God's participation in our earth walk.

We Have Lost the Sense of Inferiority

It is useless to give a paralyzed man instruction in boxing and running. The thing to do is to cure his paralysis.

As long as we are dominated by an inferiority complex, all the Sense Knowledge instruction in the way of victory and success is folly. Most of our teachers who have been trying to tell us how to win in life's fight have had nothing to give us beyond Sense Knowledge.

We have passed out of the realm of the Senses into the Realm of Revelation Knowledge, into the realm of the spirit.

We know that it is the spirit of man that conquers.

When we link that spirit up with God's Spirit, and you have a spirit dominated by God, you can conquer all the forces opposed to you.

Our Conversation

Few of us realize the effect that our conversations have upon our own spirits.

When you pretend to be what you are not and you talk glibly about it, it builds into your spirit a weakness. It is like a piece of rot in the beam of a building.

Or, your conversation may be full of discouragement, and you talk of your failures and disappointments and hard luck, until you build into your spirit-consciousness a sense of failure and inferiority. Eventually, it will rob you of initiative. You will find it difficult to rise above that mental attitude.

On the other hand, you speak the truth about what you are in Christ. You confess to your friends or your enemies what God is to you, and of your union with Him, and that you are actually partners with Him, that He is the One who backs you up and furnishes the capital to put the thing over. You give Him credit for His ability, for His wisdom, and you dare to make your confession boldly of your confidence in your success by His grace.

Remember this always. YOU RISE OR FALL TO THE LEVEL OF YOUR CONFESSION!

Called Into Fellowship with His Son

What a thrill would come to the heart if the Master should call us suddenly into counsel with Himself and the Father. That is really what He has done. He had turned the work of Redeeming the world over into our hands, and now He is asking us to fellowship Him in this work.

The instant that these facts become realities, failure is an impossibility. At once you have the consciousness of being taken out of the realm where failure dominates your life, and you come up into another realm where success is the only thing that you can think about.

You become a conqueror, a victor, an overcomer immediately in your own mind.

1 Cor. 1:9 "God is faithful, through whom ye were called into the fellowship of His Son Jesus Christ our Lord."

Everyone of us has the call to participate with Him in this realm of life.

Success in the business world is a relative term, but in the spiritual realm there is only one meaning.

It has taken some of us a long time to know that knowledge alone cannot put one over . . . simple knowledge is not enough. You must know how to use your knowledge to make it pay dividends. You must have knowledge; but more important, you must have wisdom to use that knowledge.

Multitudes have knowledge and yet are failures.

Above all your striving for knowledge, remember this fact: unless you learn how to use what you know, that knowledge simply clutters the mind. It is the ability to transform that knowledge into something, that has commercial value.

I was talking with one the other day who has several degrees from different schools and universities, but he has no ability to use his knowledge.

Experience is very valuable, but unless one has wisdom to use the knowledge that is accumulated in his experience, it has no value.

We should be very thankful for all the knowledge that we have and can get, but with the knowledge there must come the ability to utilize that knowledge.

The Secret of Wisdom

I am speaking to the believer.

God made Jesus to be our wisdom, just as He made Him to be our Righteousness, Sanctification and our Redemption. Then, if Jesus is our wisdom, how are we to use that wisdom?

The entire Redemptive program is based upon faith, and faith comes through the Word.

This Revelation that God has given us, called the Bible, is the Word of Faith.

Faith is the product of our acting intelligently upon that Word.

Jesus has been made Wisdom unto us, and we claim it and enjoy it by Faith.

Chapter The Seventeenth

HOW WISDOM COMES

E have found that wisdom cannot come from any human source. Universities cannot teach it; technical, theological schools, or schools of law cannot impart it.

The majority of people in our favored land are failures. Only about three percent of the men who go into business for themselves succeed. Seventy-five percent of marriages are failures. Only a few who have had the privilege of college and university educations make a real success of life.

This fact bothered me. I wondered why it was. Then this new unveiling of the Word came, and I saw that the difficulty lay in this: they had education, they had training, they had opportunity, but they did not know how to use the knowledge they had, or how to take advantage of the opportunity when it came, or how to fit themselves into life so they would win.

Teachers of psychoanalysis have done much to awaken thought, but they have not arrived at the real solution. Our psychologists have done able work, but, in a large measure, it has been theoretical, and has lacked the one thing that could put men over.

It is not enough to have a large fund of knowledge, we must know how to utilize it.

A manufacturer may have millions of dollars worth of goods stored in his warehouses, but unless someone has the wisdom to know how to dispose of it, it will bankrupt the manufacturer.

We have men and women who have stored up vast amounts of knowledge, just as that man has stored up his merchandise. Unless you learn how to use that stored-up knowledge, no matter what it may be worth, unless there is someone who can teach you to utilize it, you will die a failure.

We have multitudes of people who are unable to support themselves. What is the matter? It is not a lack of knowledge, but a lack of wisdom.

We are going to call wisdom the ability to make latent, accumulated knowledge worthwhile.

Since I became exercised over this problem of knowing how to use ability, talents, and acquired knowledge, I have been asking myself this question: from what source is this ability to acquire and utilize abilities?

Mr. Carnegie came here as an immigrant, but he was able to give to the world hundreds of millions of dollars. John D. Rockefeller started in poverty, and the whole world knows of his achievements. Why did he achieve, why did he win? He had wisdom. He was able to think through on his problems. While others acted emotionally, he acted wisely.

From where did that wisdom or ability to use men, circumstances and knowledge come?

It is in the spirit of man. Man is a spirit being. He is in God's class. He is in Satan's class. Satan is a spirit, as God and man are spirits.

Man's spirit only can contact God. He cannot contact God through his senses or his intellect.

Wisdom is a product of the spirit of man.

We have shown you in previous chapters of this book that there are two kinds of wisdom: one emanates primarily and basically from God, the other belongs to the god of this world, Satan. Do not forget that Satan can also contact man's spirit.

Wisdom, or the ability to use knowledge, must come from God or from Satan.

The spirit is the parent of love, hatred, joy, hope, faith, fear and courage.

Wisdom does not come from reasoning; love does not come from reasoning; joy does not come from reasoning, nor does hope. Neither does faith or courage. They are utterly independent of the reasoning faculties. They are often superior to reason.

As we go further into the study of the spirit of man, we see that all real poetry is the child of man's spirit. He will write poetry beyond reason, beyond anything which he has ever learned or anything with which he is associated. It will come bursting into his mind until it has gained the mastery.

The same is true of art. A great painting is not the work of reason, but it is the work of the spirit of man.

The architect sees his vision and dream. The great novelist is taken captive by his spirit. Inventions and creations of man are born of the spirit.

That brings us to this problem: how can we utilize this unseen, untouched force which is the very center of our being?

Developing Your Spirit Life

The secret of developing should be learned by every thinking man. He should make it his business to know how to develop his spirit nature so that he can get the most out of it.

Back behind this study lies the fact that we, who are children of God, have received into our spirits the nature and life of God. This has changed our very beings. It has linked us up with God; linked us up with wisdom, with life, with love. It has linked us up with the mightiest forces of the universe.

Jesus said, "I am the vine, ye are the branches."

Jesus is wisdom; we are a branch of wisdom. Jesus is life; we are a branch of life. Jesus is the unveiling of love; we are a branch of love.

Love is the mightiest force in the human heart, whether it be natural human love, or the new kind of love that Jesus brought to the world.

God is love, and as we walk in love, think in love, live in love, we become one with Him in His love life.

We are where we can draw on His omnipotence, His ability, His strength, His health, yes, His very life.

It is of the first importance that the child of God know what he is. Until we recognize what we really are in Christ, we will not know the riches that belong to us, and the abilities that are ours.

Can you imagine the limitlessness of an actual walk, a daily life, with the great Father God?

Can you estimate what it would mean to have an open, fresh, sweet fellowship with Him daily, so that you could meet Him on terms of utter equality, as lovers meet each other?

Such lovers haven't a single thing hidden from the object of their affection. They have abandoned themselves to love.

Can you imagine what it would mean to you if you could abandon yourself to Christ as Christ has abandoned Himself to you? Then you could understand what it would mean to be united with Him in resurrection life.

You could understand what it would mean for you to be so utterly one with Him that His victory over the adversary was your victory; thus, you would not have any combat with the enemy, because the enemy has already been defeated as far as you and Christ are concerned.

You could understand 1 Cor. 1:30, "But of Him are ye in Christ Jesus, who was made unto us wisdom from God, and righteousness, and sanctification, and redemption."

That comprehends the completed, finished work of Christ for us.

God is made wisdom in Christ to us. That means that the wisdom and ability of God is imparted to us in Christ. We have access to it.

The illustration of the vine and the branches perfectly illustrates this. The branch is a part of the vine. (He is the vine.) The vine furnishes all the life that comes up out of the ground through the roots, but the branches bear all the fruit and have the leaves and blossoms. The vine and the branch are united, they are one.

Do you see how utterly one they are? The believer is united with Christ in the same way. It is a union of life in life, of love in love, of nature in nature. You are utterly one with Him. All that He is is yours. All that you are is His.

Jesus promised the Spirit's cooperation with us in our earthly walk.

John 14:16-17 "And I will pray the Father, and He shall give you another Comforter, that He may be with you forever, even the Spirit of truth: whom the world cannot receive; for it beholdeth Him not, neither knoweth Him: ye know Him; for He abideth with you, and shall be in you."

He is called the Comforter, the Paraclete, the Teacher, and the Guide. He is called "the Spirit of truth." Truth, here, is Reality.

Physical things are real to our senses. I can touch the chair and the table. I can see the book lying in my lap. I can hear the voice of my secretary. I can feel, I can see, I can hear, I can taste, I can smell. These are all avenues through which knowledge comes to my brain. They are all real to me.

Jesus said, "I am going to send you the spirit of reality. He is going to unveil to you spiritual realities, so that they will become as tangible and real to you as material things. He is *with* you now, but a little later He is going to be *in* you."

That was fulfilled on the Day of Pentecost. He came into them. From that day, this Spirit became the teacher and the guide to lead us into reality.

John 14:26, "But the Comforter, even the Holy Spirit, whom the Father will send in my name, He shall teach you all things, and bring to your remembrance all that I said unto you."

This new Teacher is going to teach us the things of the spirit.

We know the things of the senses. They are as an open book before us. We can learn all we need to know about them. But the things of the spirit are not so real to us, so He is going to reveal Himself to us.

John 15:26, "But when the Comforter is come, whom I will send unto you from the Father, even the Spirit of Truth, which proceedeth from the Father, He shall bear witness of me."

Jesus is the unveiling of the Father, the unveiler of spiritual realities. He says that this Unseen Person is coming to unveil to us the things that made Jesus what He was in His earth walk.

"John 16:13-15, "Howbeit when He, the Spirit of Truth, is come, He shall guide you into all truth (or *reality*)."

This is really thrilling. There is coming Someone who is to live in the bodies of men, who can guide them into the reality of spiritual things.

He is going to make spiritual things as real to our spirits as physical things are real to our senses.

"He shall glorify me: for He shall take of mine, and shall declare it unto you."

All that belonged to Jesus in the spiritual realm now is to be communicated to our spirits by this Unseen Personality who is coming.

What a mighty thing it is. He says, "All things whatsoever the Father hath are mine: therefore said I, that He taketh of mine, and shall declare it unto you."

We have not grown in spirit enough yet to appreciate much of the realities of spiritual things.

You can understand now what Faith means. Faith has to do with the unseen realities. I act upon this written Word, and the unseen things become real in my spirit.

In John 14:21 Jesus said, "He that hath my commandments (that is, if we love one another as He loved us, John 13:34-35) and keepeth them, he it is that loveth me: and he that loveth me shall be loved of my Father, and I will love him, and will manifest myself unto him."

It is not going to be a manifestation that the eye can feast upon, or the hands can touch. It is going to be a spiritual unveiling, a manifestation of the very heart-life of Jesus to us.

Jesus is going to be revealed to us in the Word. As you read the Word, your heart will burn and thrill within you. Then you will be able to use the Name of Jesus.

He said, "Whatsoever ye shall ask of the Father in my name, He will give it you."

I have seen the manifestation of the Father's presence many times. I have laid hands on the sick, in the Name of Jesus, and those pains have gone and the diseases have simply ceased to be. It was the Spirit manifesting the reality of the words of Jesus.

My words are a part of me, just as God's words are a part of Him. The Word has been made real by my using it.

John 14:23, "Jesus answered and said unto him, If a man love me, he will keep my word: and my Father will love him, and we will come unto him, and make our abode with him."

If we live in the Word, and keep His Word, we will act on it. If Jesus and the Father made their home with us, that would be the very climax of love's unveiling. It would be the end of poverty and want. "My God shall supply every need of yours." He is living here with me now, living in my house, just as the Spirit has been living in my body.

When Jesus used Peter's boat to speak to the multitude, He paid Peter. He said, "Did you catch anything last night, Peter?" Peter answered, "Master, we toiled all night and caught nothing." Then the Master said, "Put out into the deep and let down your net."

Peter replied, "Master, there are no fish here, but at Thy word, I will let down the net." When he did, it was so filled with fish the nets started to break.

If He would do that for Peter, for the use of his boat, He will meet your needs. If He lives with you, it will be the end of sickness, the end of turmoil, quarrelling and bitterness. There will be no divorces in homes like that. Children will not be failures, for they will be living in constant contact with the Man of the Ages.

Notice what Jesus said, "He is with you and shall be in you." If the Holy Spirit makes His home in you, and you give Him right-of-way and treat Him as you would treat an honored guest, that house will never be filled with sickness and disease.

Isn't this beautiful? You can have God actually living in your home, in your body.

"Know ye not that your body is a temple of the Holy Spirit?" I Cor. 6:19.

That is divine cooperation with our spirits. A man who has God in him will have wisdom. At every crisis of his day's work, he has the One inside who knows all. He learns the secret of leaning back upon the One inside.

In order to develop wisdom, as it should be developed, it is going to be necessary that we have quiet hours of meditation in the Word.

Josh. 1:8 records the conversation that God had with Joshua after the death of Moses. "This book of the law shall not depart out of thy mouth, but thou shalt meditate thereon day and night, that thou mayest observe to do according to all that is written herein: for then thou shalt make thy way prosperous, and then thou shalt have good success (or *deal wisely*)."

This is the thing we want. This is the thing that will make knowledge valuable.

This is the thing that will make executives of men.

This is the thing that will make a home like heaven. The husband and wife will have wisdom to live with each other, as they rear their children.

Foolish mothers and fathers, foolish young men and women, who throw their lives away by contracting habits that will hinder them in their progress, are robbing themselves of joy in the future. The thing they most need is wisdom.

Do you think if that mother had wisdom, she would nurse a babe with a cigarette in her mouth? Do you think if that father had wisdom, he would come home drunk to a wife and baby? No! It is lack of wisdom that causes men and women to do the things they are now doing.

We might suggest a hundred ways in which we act unwisely. Do you think a man would buy property that will be a burden to him as long as he lives, if he had wisdom? No! The wise man saves his money and buys carefully. Why? Because there is something inside of him to guide him.

Can you see the value of this? It comes to our hearts as a challenge.

Do you want to cultivate this wisdom? It comes by meditation in the Word. Then your way will become prosperous. Then you will act wisely.

"Let the word of Christ dwell in you richly, teaching you, guiding you."

Meditate in Proverbs, the first eight or ten chapters, and you will see the vast place that wisdom holds. Then you will turn with excitement of soul to the Pauline Revelation to find the secret of this wisdom of which God is speaking through Solomon.

John 15:7 "If ye abide in me, and my words abide in you, ask whatsoever ye will, and it shall be done unto you."

The words of Christ are wisdom. You may commit them to memory, but that is not abiding in them. To abide in them means the Word has gained the authority over you, so you are living and walking in its wisdom. You are learning not only to obey it, but to fellowship with it. You become a partaker of the Word.

A man goes into a country and becomes a part of it. You go into the Word, and the Word becomes a part of you, and you become a part of the Word.

You learn to associate in your heart-life with the Man of Galilee, to associate your life with His Word so that you and His Word become one.

"If ye abide in me, and my words gain the supremacy in you, then you can ask anything you will and it belongs to you." Why? Because you are praying His prayer, and you are living His life.

"It is no longer I that live, but Christ liveth in me." The works that I am doing are His works. The words that I am preaching are His words. The deeds that I am doing are His deeds.

He said, "Greater works than these shall ye do; because I go unto the Father." What does He mean? He means that He is going to become so utterly one with us and we so utterly one with Him that we will have His ability, His wisdom, His authority invested in His own Name, and we will have the great, mighty Holy Spirit who raised Him from the dead dwelling in us, energizing through us.

No wonder we will do His works. We could not help but do His works. He and I have become one. It is no longer I that live, but Christ liveth in me.

Then there grows up between your heart and His heart a familiarity, an utter fellowship, just as between lovers.

The woman opens her heart to the man, the man opens his very life to her. The two lives flow into one life, and there is a new life. There is only one life now.

Christ has opened His life and you have opened your life. Your two lives flow into one. It is like two streams flowing down the mountain side. In the valley they join into one.

You learn to act on His Word in your daily life.

Prov. 3:5-6, "Trust in Jehovah with all thy heart, and lean not upon thine own understanding: in all thy ways acknowledge him, and he will direct thy paths."

Analyze this truth. Trust in Jehovah with your whole being. Stop leaning on your own understanding. You have found somebody who is wise. You are resting in Him. His ability has become your ability. His love has become your love. His strength has become your strength, and by His stripes you have found a perfect healing for spirit, soul and body.

You walk in the fulness of this wonderful heavenly union. His Word has become a part of you. You live in it.

When you need money you just remember His Word: "My God shall supply every need of yours." (Phil. 4:19.) You look up with thankfulness and say, "Father, I thank you for meeting my financial needs."

You need physical strength for some hard duty. You remember that He said He was the strength of your life.

You need wisdom and you remember that "Jehovah is my light and my salvation; whom shall I fear." Light means wisdom. Salvation means deliverance. He is my wisdom and my deliverance. I am not afraid of anything now.

The wonder and beauty of this life! This is where He and you are so tied up with each other, so utterly one with each other, that His wisdom becomes yours.

1 Cor. 1:30, "But of Him are ye in Christ Jesus." We are in Him; of His own will He brought us forth. We are His workmanship created in Christ Jesus.

Christ was made unto us wisdom from God. He is made unto us God's wisdom. He is made unto us God's righteousness, God's sanctification and redemption.

We are not common folk. This lifts us out of the common place into the super-realm. You are the real supermen and superwomen. You have gone outside of the realm of the senses, outside the realm of sense knowledge, and you have passed over into the realm of God, the spirit realm.

Eph. 3:20, "Now unto him that is able to do exceeding abundantly above all that we ask or think, according to the power that worketh in us."

God's ability is at work within you. You have grace given to you, according to the measure of the gift of Christ, so that the very ability and grace of God is yours. You will come to know the love of Christ which passes knowledge. It passes all sense evidences. You will be filled to all the fulness of God.

John 1:16, "Of His fulness we all received, and grace for grace." You have entered into His fulness, into His life. You have found the unsearchable riches of Christ. You are seated with Him at His right hand.

You died with Him; you were buried with Him. You have been raised with Him, and now you are seated with Him. You are one with Him.

You and He have found yourselves blended in each other's life. You abandon your heart-life to Him.

Perhaps there will be no test as great, but no reward as rich.

You dare trust Him with your heart. I know men and women who can trust Him with their finances, with their children, with their loved ones, with their bodies; but when it comes to trusting Him with their hearts, they balk.

If you want His wisdom, the fulness of His grace, you want to be able to say, "The Lord is my shepherd; I shall not want. He is making me to lie down in the green pastures, and He is leading me beside the waters of gentle stillness," then trust Him with your heart.

You then can say, "He has restored my soul to perfect fellowship with Himself. He has renewed my mind. He has led me out of the bondage of fear and doubt, out of the counsel of the senses, and the realm of the senses. I have come to know that my heart is safer with Him than with any one else. I love, because He loves in me, and through me. I have yielded my heart life to His Lordship."

Lying back behind this entire program is the Lordship of Love, the Lordship of the Word. You recognize His Lordship. You abandon yourself to His Lordship. It is the Lordship of Love . . . the Lordship of Wisdom. It is a lover who lords over you. Oh, what a heaven it is!

You are not afraid to love Him. You are not afraid to trust Him. You are not afraid to abandon yourself utterly to the sway of His love and of His life.

Your mind has been renewed in knowledge after the image of Him. You are coming to know His priceless will.

As this Lordship unveils itself, and you enter into the sweetness of it, there comes the last thing of which I want to speak to you: a renewed mind.

You see life from a different angle. You have a heart filled with love, with an utter abandonment to His Word, for His Word is wisdom. You recognize His indwelling presence. You have become God-inside-minded. You have become wisdom-minded.

Love and wisdom are the greatest needs of men. You have them. You have possessed them. What is the result?

1 Peter 5:7 "Casting all your anxiety upon Him, because He careth for you." You are resting in His love, in His protection and care. Fear no longer dominates you. You stand in the fulness

of His marvelous life, a victor. You are resting, while others are laboring and crying and praying in agony of failure.

You have moved out into the realm of success.

You are resting in His rest, living in His quietness.

He sat down, and you are seated with Him.

You and He now are in the sweetest companionship and fellowship.

This is success.

CHRIST MADE UNTO US WISDOM

Redemption is in the realm of the spirit. It is supernatural. It is beyond human reason to understand, without Revelation Knowledge to assist it.

When the Word tells us that Christ was made unto us wisdom, we understand that He was made unto us wisdom as He was made unto us righteousness, so that we are righteous in the Father's presence.

His Redemption is made unto us, so that we stand before the Father perfectly free from Satan and his works. Christ is made unto us Sanctification, so that we are God's separated ones.

By our accepting Christ as Saviour, and crowning Him as the Lord of our lives, we are separated from the world's dominion and the things of the world.

When we accept Christ as Saviour and confess Him as our Lord, that automatically makes Jesus our wisdom. We learn this as our minds are renewed through the Word. It becomes a natural thing for us to trust in this new kind of wisdom.

This wisdom of God was never enjoyed by natural man except on special occasions.

God gave to Solomon wisdom. He gave to Joshua wisdom. It was a special act of grace; but today, He is made wisdom to every member of the body of Christ.

Every recreated man or woman legally is a partaker of this wisdom. They may never know it and never use it, just as many have received righteousness and have never utilized the benefits from it, but this does not nullify the fact of our having wisdom.

This is the heart of it: every New Creation has the legal right to this wisdom. It belongs to him. He can use it whenever the need arises.

How can that wisdom be available? Through the Word. You meditate in the Word, actually live in the Word, and the Word will come to life for you and in you. This means that the Word is acted out in your daily life. You do the things that the Word tells you to do. You live in the Word and meditate in the Word.

You get so that you think in the Word. Your life is blended now with the *Logos,* this Living Word.

This Word contains the wisdom of God. It is the wisdom of God. It tells you what to do at every crisis.

The Spirit will make real to you what you should do. This means a God-dominated thought life, a God-dominated physical life. You will go, you will come, you will speak as the Spirit gives you utterance. There is no limit to your ability.

He imparts wisdom to those who yield themselves to His Lordship, just as God is love and God is light.

Light is wisdom. To walk in love means to walk in wisdom. If we walk in love there will be no more jangling, bitterness or unkindness; for this kind of wisdom, James tells us, "is first pure, then peaceable, gentle, easy to be entreated, full of mercy and good fruits, without *doubtfulness* or *partiality*." (marginal rendering)

It is without hypocrisy. It bears the fruit of righteousness. It leads in the paths of peace.

Can't you see that the fruit of wisdom will make our lives beautiful and Jesus-like? The fruit of wisdom is the fruit of love, for Christ is made unto us wisdom and love.

You can see there will be no bitterness, no jealousy, no hatred, no slander, no selfish taking advantage of others, but each one filled with this wisdom will walk in the highest realm of the love life.

You understand that the Holy Spirit came to give to man God's ability. He could not give man God's ability under the First Covenant because they were natural men, but now the recreated man may have God's ability.

God's very life is in him. The Holy Spirit who raised Jesus from the dead is in him.

God's nature is love, and God's love always walks in wisdom. Every step outside of love is a step in darkness and selfishness.

Wisdom, after all, is the new kind of love dominating us, for love breaks no laws; love commits no crimes. Love therefore is the fulfillment of the heart-dream of the Father for man.

James tells us how to get wisdom. The Epistle of James was written to Sense-knowledge believers. (There had to be a message especially for them.)

James 5:13-18 tells the Sense-ruled believer how to get his healing.

Peter tells us that the believer is already healed. "By His stripes ye were healed." 1 Peter 2:24.

James is talking to those who are walking by sight, by feeling, by what they hear. They are walking in the realm of the senses. They have to have the elders come and pray for them. They must hear the elders' prayer. They must feel the elders' hands upon their brow . . . then they believe.

James 1:5-7 "If any of you lacketh wisdom, let him ask of God, who giveth to all liberally and upbraideth not; and it shall be given him. But let him ask in faith, nothing doubting: for he that doubteth is like the surge of the sea driven by the wind and tossed. For let not that man think that he shall receive anything of the Lord; a doubleminded man, unstable in all his ways."

You can see that he is not talking to a believer who has entered into his inheritance. This does not match up with Eph. 1:3, "Blessed be the God and Father of our Lord Jesus Christ, who hath blessed us with every spiritual blessing in the heavenly places in Christ."

There we see the believer who has entered into all his privileges, walking in all the fulness of the wisdom of Christ.

This one to whom James refers is walking in sense knowledge. His faith ebbs and flows. The babe in Christ is not overlooked. He is yet carnal; that is, he is ruled by the senses, he walks as a common man. The world pleasures have to satisfy him, he has not yet reached a place where he is satisfied with the Lord. In great grace, the Lord says to him, "If any of you lack wisdom . . ."

I would that all could understand this. *Wisdom belongs to the believer.* It is not a problem of faith. It is one who is living as though he were out of Christ that lacks wisdom; and having no sense of righteousness, no sense of his relationship, he is driven now by his great need to pray for wisdom. He is trying to exercise faith for this wisdom. He does not know that all that Christ did and is today belongs to him. What belongs to him requires no faith to enjoy.

Not knowing that the riches of grace are his, and that he is blessed with every spiritual blessing in Christ, he comes in his simplicity of ignorance and prays for faith.

We always need faith when we pray for something that does not belong to us, and we are not sure of getting it; but we do not need faith for a thing that we already possess, something that already belongs to us.

Let the babe still pray for faith, but you who are mature do not need to, for Jesus is your faith. He was made unto you faith.

It is so important that the heart grasp this clearly, for wisdom belongs to you as much as Jesus belongs to you, as much as His intercession belongs to you.

Jesus' intercession belongs to you. He ever lives to make intercession for you. It is not a problem of your faith, it is a problem of your acting on the Word and enjoying the privileges that belong to you.

As long as you pray for faith, it indicates that the thing you are praying for does not belong to you, and you are trying to make God give you something that is not yours. But, all that Christ is, is yours. All He did is yours. All He will do tomorrow is yours. It is not a problem of faith.

John 1:16, "Of His fulness have we all received, and grace upon grace."

You have received of His fulness. Whether or not you have enjoyed what you have received, is not the problem. It is yours. It is set to your account. It is more than that, it is in you.

The problem that confronts you, is to learn to take your place as a son, and enjoy the fulness of the riches of His grace. It all belongs to you!

SOME PEOPLE WHO LACKED WISDOM

In Genesis 25:29-34 is a story of a foolish young man, an heir to the Abrahamic Blood Covenant. He was a thoughtless, careless type of individual who cared more for a meal or a physical pleasure than he did for eternal things.

In a fit of despondency he sold his birthright for a single meal. The food was red beet hash. It was called Edom, meaning *red*, and that name was given to him, a name of derision, a name that indicated his folly . . . Edom.

He is a type of those who, today, sell their birthright of success and usefulness for a little physical pleasure. They have ability, they have knowledge, but they seem to be unable to use their ability and knowledge wisely.

They do not have the wisdom to use knowledge.

The story of Samson, the superman, in Judges 13:16-27, reveals to us another example. There was no man in his class. He had physical strength, he had knowledge, but he lacked the one thing that puts men over the top — wisdom.

He was a superman. He was in the First Covenant with all its possibilities. The ability of God was at his disposal.

He had God's protection and God's blessing upon him.

He dared to take advantage of his Covenant rights, and became the strongest man the world ever knew. But withal, he was a failure.

Samson's name might have gone down through the ages as the outstanding product of the Abrahamic Covenant, but he was a failure. He committed suicide in order to get revenge upon his captors.

Look at him, the blind hero in captivity. God's leader for that age, a captive!

How many men are like that today. Satan has blinded them; their spiritual eyes are put out; they seem to have no wisdom to know the right thing to do.

Esau failed. History might have read, "The God of Abraham, the God of Isaac, and the God of Esau," but he lacked wisdom.

Ahithophel, prime minister of Israel under David, was the wisest man of his age, but he lacked wisdom at the crisis; and then in shame and discomfiture committed suicide.

How Daniel's wisdom shines out through the dark pages of human history. While Israel was in captivity, Daniel sought God and found wisdom.

Wisdom comes from God. Only God can give it (the kind of wisdom of which we speak).

There are three kinds of wisdom: natural human wisdom, satanic wisdom, and Divine Wisdom.

The name of Judas Iscariot could have come ringing down through the ages today, as one of the great leaders of the Apostolic band, but he lacked wisdom. He sold Jesus for thirty pieces of silver. Those pieces of silver that he could hold in his hand seemed greater to him than the privilege of being a companion of John and Peter and James and the others.

How differently history would read had Judas possessed wisdom.

Jesus gives us some pictures of the unwise.

In Luke 12:13-31 is the story of the rich man. He had marvelous ability. He must have had great knowledge. He had accumulated for himself great wealth. Instead of going to God and getting the plan for his life, he plays the fool.

Matt. 7:24-27 is the story of the foolish man who built his house upon the sand.

All down through the ages we have had these foolish men. Wisdom belonged to them, they could have claimed it.

You who read this book can have God's wisdom in every crisis of your life.

You can be known as a wise man, a wise woman; or you can foolishly build your house upon the sand, and when the storm comes and beats down upon it, all your life's struggles and efforts go down with a crash!

Matt. 25:1-13 is the story of the unwise virgins. These virgins are not the Church. They are the bridesmaids of the Church. They didn't have oil in their lamps. They didn't invite the Spirit to guide them in life. They had the wisdom of the world, but they did not seek wisdom of God. They were foolish. They had every opportunity, but they didn't take advantage of it.

In Rev. 3:14-42 is a picture of the unwise Church. This is the period in which we are living now. The Church could just as well govern the morality of our nation.

If the Church were awake, there would be no taverns and bars to damn and blight our young men and women.

If the Church had wisdom, the wave of lawlessness and crime would end.

Jesus was made unto the Church wisdom, but she has gloried in her sense knowledge. She has laughed at the wisdom of God, and she is paying an awful price for it.

The Church is suffering today for the lack of wisdom.

Chapter The Eighteenth

EXACT KNOWLEDGE

T goes without argument that God has the ability to give us exact knowledge in regard to spiritual things.

We believe that the Word contains this exact knowledge in all spiritual wisdom that is necessary for our growth and development so that we may know and do the will of the Father perfectly.

Sense Knowledge is born of experience and experiments. It is never perfect. It always has an element of limitation, for no one is ever positive about his experiments. There is always a chance of a mistake, because this knowledge comes through the avenues of the Senses.

My sight may be defective, so that I cannot be positive that the thing is as it has appeared. Or, if I have depended upon my hearing, I am not sure that I have heard aright. Or, if it came through the sense of touch, I am not certain of it. There is always the possibility of misunderstanding.

We little appreciate the tremendous effort that has been expended on gaining the knowledge that we have in the realm of mechanics, mathematics, metallurgy, chemistry, medicine and the other sciences.

The Greek word "epignosis" is translated by Thayer "correct," or "precise knowledge."

Young translates it "full knowledge."

That means exact, complete, correct, precise knowledge.

"For this cause we also, since the day we heard it, do not cease to pray and make request for you, that ye may be filled with the knowledge of His will in all spiritual wisdom and understanding."

Paul's prayer is that they might be filled with the exact, the precise, the full knowledge of His will in all spiritual wisdom and understanding.

167

The Spirit does not suggest possibilities that are unobtainable. If Paul prayed that the believers at Colosse should have this kind of knowledge, we believe it was possible for them to have it.

In the tenth verse he says, "To walk worthily of the Lord." That was the object of this full knowledge.

"To walk worthily of the Lord, unto all pleasing, bearing fruit in every good work, and increasing in the exact or full knowledge of God."

That knowledge is here in the Word, and Jesus promised that when the Comforter came He would guide us into all truth, that He would give to us a revelation of the Father's will.

We know that He gave to Paul a revelation of the finished work of Christ.

We know that we have a revelation of what Jesus did from the time He was made sin on the cross and died, until He arose from the dead, carried His blood into the Heavenly Holy of Holies, and was accepted as our Substitute.

His work was accepted as a perfect Redemption for us. He sat down at the Right Hand of the Majesty on High, because He had completed the Redemption that met every demand of Justice, and every need of man.

1 Cor. 2:12 is a challenge to every one of us. "But we received not the spirit of the world, but the spirit which is from God; that we might know the things that were freely given to us of God."

You see, we have a right to know the things that have been freely given to us in the Redemptive work of Christ. They are of no value unless we know them.

Col. 3:10 is a suggestion of the Father's heart desire toward us. "And have put on the new man, that is being renewed unto knowledge after the image of Him that created him."

Notice carefully that the New Birth is "putting on the new man." When we are Born Again, it is our spirits that are recreated. Then the Spirit, through the Word, renews our minds, and that renewal brings us into fellowship with the Father.

Adam was created, spiritually and intellectually, in the image and likeness of God. When Adam fell, his mind became darkness.

2 Cor. 4:4 "In whom the god of this world hath blinded the minds of the unbelieving, that the light of the gospel of the glory of Christ, who is the image of God, should not dawn upon them."

This tells us that the god of this world has blinded the minds of the unbelieving that they may not know the true God, or spiritual things. The natural mind is blinded to the knowledge of supernatural things.

1 Cor. 2:14 "Now the natural man receiveth not the things of the Spirit of God; for they are foolishness unto him; and he cannot know them, because they are spiritually understood."

There are certain things that the natural man can know about Revelation. He can understand the Spirit's great argument in the book of Romans in regard to God's Redemption for man.

The first eight chapters of Romans are written in the realm of Sense Knowledge, so that Sense Knowledge man can know how to become a child of God. But he cannot understand Ephesians, Philippians, and Colossians, which were given that we, as Believers, should be led into all the knowledge of our rights and privileges in Christ."

For instance, Col. 1:12 says, "Giving thanks unto the Father, who made us meet (or gave us the ability) to enjoy our share of the inheritance of the saints in light."

Every child of God has the ability to know the Word, whether he recognizes it or not, for Jesus said, "Howbeit when He, the Spirit of truth, is come, He shall guide you into all the truth." John 16:13.

The Spirit of truth was to guide us into the Reality, into the fulness of our privileges in Christ. He was to take the things of Christ, that were wrought for us in the great Substitutionary Sacrifice, and make them real in our lives.

He was not only to make it historically clear through the Revelation that was given to Paul, but He was to make it experimentally real in every believer's life who sought to know and enjoy its fulness.

You remember in Col. 1:9, that we have referred to before, that He says, "That ye may be filled with the exact knowledge of His will in all spiritual wisdom and understanding." That is the Spirit's prayer for the church. Every one who desires this knowledge may have it.

"Bearing fruit in every good work and increasing in this exact knowledge." This is to me an amazing statement.

Eph. 4:7, "But unto each one of us was the grace given according to the measure of the gift of Christ." Now, every one of us has grace to enter into all the riches of our inheritance.

John 1:16 intimates this. "Of His fulness have we all received and grace upon grace."

The reason that He says, "grace upon grace" is that our hearts shrink from the fact that this fulness, this completeness, this perfectness of Christ has become ours. His grace is there, and it is "grace upon grace" that is going to enable us to enter into all that belongs to us.

In Eph. 4:11-13 He declares that the church has apostles, prophets, evangelists, pastors and teachers. "For the perfecting of the saints unto the work of ministering, unto the building up of the body of Christ: till we all attain unto the unity of faith and the unity of knowledge of the Son of God, unto a full-grown man, unto the measure of the stature of the fulness of Christ."

You see, it is the desire of the Father that we should graduate from this higher university of spiritual knowledge, that we may be able to bring forth fruit unto the praise of His glory, and that we may walk worthily of the Lord, unto all pleasing.

It does not glorify Him for us to be buffeted about by every wind of doctrine, by the power of the enemy.

His heart is set on full-knowledge men and women who will be able to stand against the cunning artifices of the Adversary, able to pray the prayer of faith for the sick and the needy, and able to unveil the Word of His grace to those who are hungry for spiritual things.

1 Tim. 2:4 intimates the Father's desire for His children. "Who would have all men to be saved, and come to this perfect, this precise, and exact knowledge of the truth."

Not only that they may be saved, but that they may grow in Christ; that they may spiritually come to full age so that the Word will become a living reality to them, and that prayer will not be begging, but a joyful cooperation with the Father.

We are taking Jesus' place here on the earth, and prayer should be simply a conference with the Father, laying before Him the needs of men and women about us. Our prayers will be a requisition for food, healing and strength for those in need.

We will not be as those mentioned in 2 Tim. 3:7 who are ever learning but never able to come to the full knowledge of truth, or of the reality of the Word.

There are those who are just flitting from one church to another, from one Bible teacher to another, dabbling in this course and in that, but never settling down and becoming proficient as teachers of the Word and helpers of those who are in need.

I believe that it is the Father's will that we have an exact knowledge of His will. We will become exact, precise, full-knowledge teachers of the Word. That means more than just what our church or our creed has accepted. (How few well-rounded teachers of the Word there are!)

If I am a Methodist, or Baptist, or Presbyterian, or if I belong to the Pentecostal folk, I can only teach the message that their creed permits. Anything outside of that is questionable.

You see, we have locked Christ up in a creed, so that He is no bigger than our creed will allow Him to be. We have made it impossible for Him to help folk beyond the limit of our doctrines. This is very unfortunate.

One body of believers, that has given to the church perhaps more truth than any other one sect, has closed the doors against any further knowledge than that which they possessed a hundred years ago; so it is impossible to help them.

The old line denominations that have creeds, written or unwritten, have not admitted a new truth in fifty years. They have nothing but the things that their forefathers gave them.

In the realm of science, mechanics, and the arts, there has been marvelous development and growth. Chemistry has revolutionized the modern world, but Christianity has lain utterly dormant. No one among the leaders has dared to go beyond their creeds, for if they do, the leaders will read them out of their denomination. This is unfortunate.

In Heb. 10:26 we have a significant warning. "For if we sin wilfully after that we have received the full knowledge of the truth, there remaineth no more a sacrifice for sin." (That means exact, precise, full knowledge of the truth.)

This wilful sin is the denial of the deity of Jesus and the denial of the blood of the New Covenant wherewith He was sanctified, calling it the blood of a common man.

That is the only unpardonable sin, and it can only be committed by those who have come to a full knowledge of the truth.

A babe in Christ may prattle about the things he doesn't believe, but he is only a babe, and it is the prattle of an infant in Christ. It is unfortunate that he talks as he does, but the Father understands it and forgives him.

There isn't much danger of anyone who has received the full knowledge of the truth ever denying the substitutionary sacrifice of Christ.

In 2 Peter 1:2 He says, "Grace to you and peace be multiplied in the exact, the perfect knowledge of God and of Jesus our Lord." This is a wonderful invocation.

Grace and peace be multiplied in this full knowledge, this full revelation of the Father and our Lord Jesus. How that would revolutionize the church! How that would revolutionize your life!

The third verse, "Seeing that His divine power hath granted unto us all things that pertain unto life and godliness, through the knowledge of Him that called us by His own glory and virtue."

Exact knowledge would not be demanded unless it could be attained.

We have a perfect Revelation. We have a perfect Teacher, the Holy Spirit. The Father chose His own instrument, the Apostle Paul, a man who could receive a perfect Revelation from God and not adulterate it with his own philosophy.

It was necessary that we have exact knowledge of the Father's will so that we might be well pleasing to Him.

He gave to us a perfect New Creation, imparting His nature to our spirits. He made Jesus to be our wisdom, the Holy Spirit to be our teacher, and this Revelation to be our text book. In this text book we have His exact will revealed.

You remember that Paul said the Revelation was not of man nor through man. Sense Knowledge did not color it nor rob it of its perfection.

This absolute knowledge builds faith and assurance in our Redemption.

Chapter The Nineteenth

WHAT BELONGS TO US IN CHRIST

ALLOW me to enumerate some of the great blessings that belong to us now.

We have the opportunity of tying up with Omnipotence. We may utilize the vast resources of the God of the Universe.

How it thrilled me what I first saw what could become ours today. I remember, years ago I came in contact with a young man who had, through peculiar circumstances, been able to join one of the most outstanding financial institutions in America. How the other young men of his age coveted such a privilege. Some of them almost resented his success. Today I can see how a young man can tie up with God and get into the organization of the Universe.

We have been startled at the power revealed in the Atomic Bomb, but this is something greater. You will be tied up with the Creator of the element that made that bomb.

Think of receiving Eternal Life, the nature of God Almighty. You come into His family and partake of His Divine Nature. You are as near to Him in your relationship as Jesus was in His earth walk.

When you become a partaker of His nature, you instantly become a sharer in His ability. You can stand in His presence, you can fellowship with Him. You become the righteousness of God in Christ.

You can stand in the presence of God without the sense of guilt or condemnation. You can stand in the presence of Satan and all of his hosts without any sense of inferiority. You become an absolute master of the Satanic forces.

You remember that Jesus said, "In my name ye shall cast out demons." That is for this age. That is now.

He offers you the opportunity of taking the place of the absent Master. With the authority of His Name, you become Heaven's representative.

You not only have God's nature, but Jesus says that He is going to send the Holy Spirit who will make His home in your body, if you will invite Him in.

1 John 4:4, "Ye are of God my little children; Greater is He that is in you than he that is in the world."

What does this mean? It means that you are actually of God. Born of Him, in His Family, and because of that, the great Holy Spirit, who raised Jesus from the dead, is willing to take up His abode in you.

He will take you over. He will become your sponsor in this new wonderful life. It is as though He stood by your side and whispered, "If you will allow me, I will come in and teach you how to let me think with your mind so you will have the very mind of Christ."

Your daily walk will reflect the mind of Christ. The Father's will will become your will. You will be filled with the very love nature of the Father. The Holy Spirit will build into you all of those beautiful characteristics that you have admired in Jesus, until they dominate your life.

You cannot be a failure when you let the Holy Spirit loose in you. You cannot be defeated if you give Him the dominance, and the rule of your life.

I remember when He spoke to me, and I said, "Master, if I should recognize your Lordship, your dominion over me, you would make me preach to the men and women of the "skidroad." I cannot do that, I want to have a beautiful church."

Then He whispered, "Don't you know that I love you more than you love yourself? I am more ambitious for your success than you are."

My spirit was hushed. I couldn't keep the tears back. I whispered brokenly, "Master, I see it. I recognize your Lordship. I will walk where you guide."

Then I discovered that my union with Him made me big. You see, it is a wonderful thing. You have God dwelling in you. It is more than wonderful, it passes all reason. It sweeps one out into omnipotence where you cast all your cares and anxieties upon Him for He careth for you.

You remember Romans 8:31-36 . . . "If God is for you who can be against you?"

You, who are starting out in life, here is an opportunity to tie up with the One who can make you a success, give you the thing that your heart has craved.

Hear Him whisper, "If God is for you, who is against you?"

You unconsciously change it and say, "God is with me, and I fear no one."

I remember, "He that spared not His own Son but delivered Him up for us all, how shall He not also with Him freely give us all things?"

It has become personal now. It is not "us," it is "me." It is no longer the human race, it is "me." It is no longer the Body of Christ, it is for "me" individually. I am the man. I have Him freely as only love can give freely.

Then I remembered Eph. 1:3, "Blessed be the God and Father of my Lord Jesus Christ, who has blessed me with every spiritual blessing in the heavenlies in Christ." Notice, He does not say, "*can* bless me" (if I have faith). Not, "*will* bless me," but "*has* blessed me." I AM BLESSED! My every need is met.

One can hardly take it in. The riches of Christ are mine.

Did you notice the next sentence? "Who can lay anything to the charge of God's elect? It is God that has justified."

You may have enemies that will fight you, but they can bring no charge against you that will separate you from His love. Why? Because Jesus is your Advocate. He is the family lawyer. He is your personal lawyer. He is the One who ever lives to make Intercession for you.

When the enemy trips you, and you do something unwise, you look up and whisper, "Father, forgive me in Jesus' Name." Your Advocate is there at the Father's right hand, and He pleads your case and your fellowship is restored.

"I write unto you little children that ye sin not, and if any man sin we have an advocate with the Father, Jesus Christ the righteous." 1 John 2:1.

The moment your Advocate makes an appeal for you, everything is cleared up. You stand in the Father's presence as though sin had never been.

When the Father forgives He forgets, and He wants you to forget too.

Did you ever notice that thirty-fourth verse, "Who is he that condemneth? It is Christ Jesus that died for you."

Would Christ condemn you? No, never. Why He ever lives to make Intercession for you. He is your Lord Advocate. He is the One who loved you and gave Himself up for you. He vouches for you. He stands for you, and in all of life's battles, He backs you up. He gives you His ability and His wisdom. You are linked up with Him. You are His earthly representative.

I wonder if you have ever realized your legal rights in Christ?

You see, Christianity is a legal document. The Bible is made up of two legal books. They are the old and the new Covenants.

A Covenant is a contract. The first contract was between Abraham and Jehovah. The second Contract is between Jesus and the Father.

The Israelites were the beneficiaries of the first Covenant. The New Creation folk are the beneficiaries of the New Covenant.

The blood of Jesus Christ is the red seal upon the document of the New Covenant. On the basis of that, God is able, on legal grounds, to give Eternal Life to man. God legally gives Eternal Life, His own nature, to every one who takes Christ as Savior and confesses Him as Lord of their life. They legally become His child. They have the legal right to invite the Holy Spirit to come into their body. They have a legal right to the use of the Name of Jesus.

That Name has all authority in the three worlds. (Read my book, "The Wonderful Name of Jesus.")

Remember when Jesus said, "All authority has been given to me in heaven and on earth, go ye therefore and make students of all nations, and lo, I am with you alway."

"I am there in My Name and in My Word, and in the Person of the Holy Spirit. You are never left alone. I want you to know that I am the vine and ye are the branches. Wherever the branch goes, the vine life flows. The branch may be in Africa, India, or China; the vine life follows it. You and I are insolubly united. We are one. That Holy union was made by the life of the Father."

This is a picture of the marvelous union between the Father, Son, and believer.

From today, plan to walk with the consciousness of His being your Father and you being His child. You are doing His work; you are His representative.

The "lo, I am with you alway" was spoken to you personally. He is with you in the living Word as you speak it and live it in your daily life. See what He is doing? He is taking the Word, which is the nature of the Father, and He is building it into your spirit life. He is making that Word a part of yourself.

Now you can face whatever arises, because you have a legal right to the use of that Name.

Peter said, "In the Name of Jesus Christ, arise and walk," to the cripple at the beautiful gate of the Temple.

Paul commanded that evil spirit to leave the girl in the Name of Jesus, and it left.

That Name has all authority today, and you have the ability to use that Name. It is for you personally. You may use it in your daily combat with the forces that surround you. This Name makes you more than a conqueror in every field.

It is not going to be difficult for you to take advantage of this, because these things belong to you. They are yours the moment you become a child of God. Only one who is united with Deity can enjoy these privileges.

The ability of God the Father is yours. The wisdom of the Master is yours. You have everything that heaven can give you.

"But," you say, "I do not see anyone living this life."

That does not discredit the Word, does it? Most of the people have not seen the truth and reality of it. They have not known what it means.

We have come to a crisis in human history, where common things will not meet the issue. No common thing could meet the atomic bomb, only something in its own class can meet it.

Your combat is not against flesh and blood, but it is against the principalities and powers.

The Lord made provisions for this fight. If you are a child of God, you are more than a conqueror in every crisis.

Dare to believe His Word, act the part, and take your place today!

Chapter The Twentieth

COUNTING ON THE ABILITY OF GOD IN YOU

HOW well I remember the years I sought for power with God, prayed for power, and read every book I could find that would tell me how to get it.

One day Phil. 2:13 opened up to me. I was reading it in the Twentieth Century Translation. "For it is God who is at work within you, willing and working His own good pleasure."

I wondered why I had never seen it before. I had the Power House in me. I had the Spirit who raised Jesus from the dead, and I had never recognized Him!

I found that I had been governed by experiences. I believed that power would come if I had a certain kind of experience. I sought for that experience. I found that I had more confidence in the experiences of others than in the Word.

Then I saw that if God's ability were let loose in me, it would perform the prodigies my heart was set upon.

I had never majored the fact that I had God in me. I had never majored the fact that the Word on my lips would do the same thing that it did on the lips of Jesus and the disciples.

Then I saw this truth; the Holy Spirit was in me to give me the ability to use the Name and the Word.

This Name has all authority in it. You remember Jesus said, "Whatsoever you ask of the Father in my Name, He will give you."

And again, "In my Name ye shall cast out demons, speak in new tongues, lay hands on the sick and they shall recover."

Notice this carefully, "that whatsoever ye ask in my Name I will do it."

The miracle working ability of God is in that Name.

I had never before heard anyone preach on it. I will never forget how timid I was when I tried that Name the first time. How thrilled I was when I saw that it worked. It did the thing.

After a while I dared to stand before a congregation and in that Name set the people free from Satan and see them intelligently accept Jesus Christ as their Saviour.

I did it at first with individuals, and then with an entire congregation. How easy it became to give the invitation. It seemed as if I had lifted a cloud that hung over them.

I saw that I was dealing with supernatural issues. I had dominion over the forces of Darkness in the Name of Jesus. I did not need to pray for power, all I needed was authority, and that authority was in the Name.

Then one day 1 Cor. 1:30 dawned upon me with a new clearness. "God made Jesus wisdom unto us." The ability and wisdom Jesus used in His earth walk was mine.

No one had ever taught us the difference between wisdom and knowledge. No one had ever told us about the authority that the Father had vested in the Name of Jesus. No one had ever preached on our rights and privileges as sons and daughters, and of our right to the use of His Name.

All of this time there was an undercurrent in my life, a sense of unworthiness. The Adversary seemed to delight in making me conscious of unworthiness.

I tried everything that man had taught. I sought the "clean heart," "entire Sanctification," "Second Work of Grace," everything that was preached. I was blessed for a while, but it would all fade away. I wanted something that was permanent. I knew I could find it in the Word.

I was reading Romans 3:26. I knew that the key word of Romans was "Righteousness," but I had no definite interpretation of Righteousness. I had always thought it meant right conduct, right living. I did not see the Pauline significance of it.

In the Pauline Epistles we see that the word Righteousness means the ability to stand in the presence of the Father without any sense of guilt, fear, or condemnation; and in the presence of Satan without any sense of inferiority or fear.

The problem was how to get that righteousness.

Romans 3:26 solved that issue. Let me give you the American Revised Marginal Rendering of it. "That He might Himself be Righteous, the Righteousness of him who has faith in Jesus."

Strange, I had never seen it before. God Himself was to become my Righteousness the moment that I accepted Christ and confessed Him as my Lord.

Then I remembered Romans 10:10 "For with the heart man believeth unto Righteousness, and with the mouth confession is made unto salvation."

Then 2 Cor. 5:21, "Him who knew no sin God made to become sin that we might become the Righteousness of God in Him."

I couldn't believe it at first. I struggled for days and days on this scripture. I knew that if I became the Righteousness of God in Christ that I would never again depend upon experiences.

I had arrived. The thing that my heart had craved was here, but it would never become real to me until I confessed it before the world.

That Sunday morning, when I dared to say "I am the Righteousness of God in Christ," was when I experienced what it meant. A strange quietness filled my whole being. A joy that I had never before experienced, filled my heart.

I said unconsciously, "I have arrived. I have it. Now I can approach the Father without the sense of unworthiness. I can face the Adversary as a master."

I remember that afternoon, we had a service. As I was coming up the steps to the church, I said, "Satan, at last you are my servant. I am your master."

I had never had that consciousness before. I had been preaching for many years, but I had never known that I was the Righteousness of God in Christ. I had never realized what I had in me.

Now I said, "Father, I am going to let the Spirit loose, He shall be free in me."

Now I could use this Word, the Sword of the Spirit, as I had never before used it.

Then it was that I saw the very genius of Christianity. God had Recreated me. He had given me Eternal Life. He had made me His Righteousness in Christ, by imparting to me His own nature.

I had never realized it, never understood it, consequently I had never taken advantage of it.

God had greatly blessed my ministry, He had marvelously opened the Word to me, but this avenue of ministry had never dawned on me. Why? Because no one preached it. No one told us about it. We had unconsciously locked Jesus, the Word, and the Holy Spirit, up in our Creeds and Doctrines.

Now I had a living Word, a miracle-performing Word on my lips.

I will never forget an experience I had. I was called to a neighboring town to pray for an insane man. When I went into the room where he was, his mother introduced me to him. He turned his back to me and would not speak. Like a flash, the truth dawned upon me. I was the Righteousness of God in Christ. I had the superiority over the forces of darkness. I stepped up to the man, and in the Name of Jesus, I demanded the demons to come out of him, and never return.

It wasn't a minute before he grasped my hand, and we had the sweetest fellowship the rest of the visit.

How his mother rejoiced. In the Name of Jesus her son had been set free.

I had the ability to use His Name, and had never before realized it.

A few days later I was called to pray for a young man who had been injured in the first war. I sat by his side opening the Word to him. When I was ready to leave, he asked me to pray for a pain he had in the back of his head.

I again used that Name. I remembered what I was in Christ.

The next day I went back and found him sitting up in a chair. I prayed again for him for perfect deliverance. I knew nothing of his condition. I did not ask him to get up, I prayed for him and left.

The next night I was attending our prayer service. As I entered the door, a young man spoke to me. I greeted him and started into the building. He called me back and asked if I didn't remember him.

His face was familiar, but I did not place him. He said, "I am the fellow you prayed for yesterday. I was shell shocked in the war and hadn't walked for years. Look what I can do now."

Tears filled my eyes, as I watched him jump and bend his body in every direction with no pain. He was perfectly healed.

You see, I had found my level. I had seen a great many people healed before that, but at last I had found my place in the program of God.

I was the Righteousness of God in Christ. I had the legal right to the use of His Name. I had Him inside of me who was greater than any force that could come against me.

A few days after that, I was invited to go to the hospital and pray for a woman. This woman had been a teacher in Unity.

I unfolded the Word to her and she accepted Christ. I prayed for her and left. The next night she was in my services, perfectly healed. She became one of our strongest helpers.

I had learned how to take advantage of what I really had in Christ.

We are linked up with God. He is now our own very Father. We are utterly one with Him.

He is in us. We are in Him.

He is a part of us. We are a part of Him.

We are His children by nature. We are born of Heaven.

We are begotten of the Holy Spirit. The Word has given us life. "Of His own will He brought us forth."

This union with the Master and with the Father is beyond human intelligence.

The natural mind cannot grasp it.

We stand in the presence of it, beggared of the ability to fathom it, and yet it is ours.

We are tied up with Him. We are partakers of His nature. We are born of His Spirit. We are indwelt by His Word. We are kept by His grace. We are controlled by His love.

What more could you ask?

Chapter The Twenty-first

GOD-INSIDE-MINDED

THIS is one of the greatest facts of Revelation, one of the most important to the believer, and one of the most precious to the love-ruled heart.

The New Testament gives us three relations that God sustains toward man: first, God *for* us; second, God *with* us; and third, God *in* us.

To have God for us guarantees success. "If God is for us, who can be against us?" If God is on our side, we are sure to win.

If God is for you, and you know it, you become utterly fearless. No matter how foreboding, how difficult the situation may be, you are calmly assured that you must win.

There can be no defeat if He, the great unseen, is with us.

Romans 8:31, "If God is for us, who is against us?" To have God with you is to walk with Love. It is the arm-in-arm walk with the Man of the ages. You have the consciousness that He is not only for you, but that in every place in life, He is with you.

No matter what the circumstances may be, your Lord is with you.

How the knowledge of this fact lifts the heart, how it buoys us up with confidence.

John 14:23, "If a man love me, he will keep my Word: and my Father will love ·him, and we will come unto him, and make our abode with him." Jesus and the Father will live with us in our home! What a protected and quiet place it will be!

John 14:16,17, Jesus said, "I will pray the Father, and He shall give you another Comforter, that He may be with you for ever, even the Spirit of truth: whom the world cannot receive; for it beholdeth Him not, neither knoweth Him: ye know Him; for He abideth with you, and shall be in you."

The Spirit was with them in Christ, but the hour was coming when Christ would go away and the Spirit would make His

185

home not only with them, but actually in them, making their bodies His temple.

This is one of the richest of all the truths about Him.

Acts 2:1-4, we read of the Holy Spirit's coming into the upper room and filling it with Himself, so that the disciples were immersed in Him.

They saw tongues of fire upon each other's heads, typical of the way the message of the good news was to be proclaimed by tongues of fire, anointed of the Spirit.

Then it declares that they were all filled with the Holy Spirit.

First, He immersed them, then He manifested Himself upon their foreheads, then He came into their bodies.

Immersion or Baptism in the Holy Spirit is not indwelling. You can be immersed in water and not have water in you.

You can be Baptized in the Holy Spirit and not receive the Holy Spirit as an indweller.

Baptism in the Holy Spirit is the hour of the New Birth.

1 Cor. 12:13 (literal translation) "For in one Spirit were we all immersed into one body."

They began to speak with other tongues as the Spirit gave them utterance. The tongues were not the evidence of His indwelling, they needed no outward manifestation to prove that. He had come in to make His home in their bodies.

Now the message they preached would be their evidence; their godly lives that followed, and their love walk, demonstrated His indwelling presence.

It was a wonder day. It was man's great day, when God glorified those humiliated bodies and came into them to make them His home.

Phil. 3:21, "Who shall fashion anew the body of our humiliation, that it may be conformed to the body of His glory, according to the working whereby He is able even to subject all things unto Himself."

Sin humiliated our bodies, making them mortal, subject to disease and death. Now, the Holy Spirit glorifies them by making them His home. God at last is making man's Satan-ruled body His temple.

1 Cor. 6:19 "Or know ye not that your body is the temple of the Holy Spirit which is in you, which ye have from God? and ye are not your own; for ye were bought with a price: glorify God therefore in your body."

This is one of the most solemn truths of the great revelation, that God makes Himself the companion of every act of our lives.

He comes into our bodies to make them His pulpit, and to make our lips His mouthpiece through which He is going to give a message of love to the world.

Phil. 1:20 gives us a little more light on this subject: "But that with all boldness, as always, so now also Christ shall be magnified in my body whether by life, or by death. For to me to live is Christ, and to die is gain."

Gal. 2:20, "It is no longer I that live, but Christ liveth in me."

How little the church has made of this fact. There is no fact about the Redemption that is to me so utterly marvelous. It is a miracle of Grace, an act of love transcending anything except Calvary.

God is actually making His home in our bodies.

Only a few of us are conscious of God in our bodies. You hear men constantly talking about their lack of power, and lack of ability.

He planned that we should not think of what we are going to say when we are compelled to give our witness, but that He, Himself, through our lips, would make the great confession.

Matt. 10:19-20, "But when they deliver you up, be not anxious, how or what ye shall speak: for it shall be given you in that hour what ye shall speak. For it is not ye that speak, but the Spirit of your Father that speaketh in you."

How little we have appreciated this. How few of us have dared to let Him loose in us and give Him His freedom. The Holy Spirit is to speak in you, to take you over.

We know that spiritualists and mediums yield themselves to the unclean spirits and that they take them over and speak strange things through them.

Why can't we be taken over by the Holy Spirit so that He will speak through us an unadulterated message, fresh from the heart of the Father.

To most of us, the indwelling truth is but a dogma instead of a reality. It is just a doctrine that we talk about, not a great fact that causes us to rejoice.

Col. 1:29 tells us how the Spirit wrought in the apostle Paul. "Whereunto I labor also, striving according to His working, which worketh in me mightily," or "with ability."

Paul was God-inside-minded. He knew that in him was the Spirit whom Jesus had promised should guide them into all reality.

He knew that the Spirit who raised Jesus from the dead had made His home in his body. He knew that that Spirit could heal the sick and raise the dead, and bless the multitudes with messages that would produce faith and the New Birth.

He knew that the Omnipotent One was dwelling in him, and he dared yield himself to the sway of that mighty One.

Eph. 3:20, "Now unto Him that is able to do exceeding abundantly above all that we ask or think according to the power that worketh in us."

He is able to do in us and through us, things beyond our comprehension. This is one of the most blessed truths. How we ought to yield ourselves utterly to the sway of this indwelling One.

If the Spirit who raised Jesus from the dead is in you, you become a limitless possibility in your community.

Eph. 1:19-23, "What the exceeding greatness of His power to us-ward who believe, according to that working of the strength of His might which He wrought in Christ, when He raised Him from the dead, and made Him to sit at His right hand in the heavenly places, far above all rule, and authority, and power, and dominion, and every name that is named, not only in this age, but also in that which is to come: and He put all things in subjection under His feet and gave Him to be head over all things to the church, which is His body, the fulness of Him that filleth all in all."

You get a picture here of the Omnipotence of God, of the utter greatness of God, and that greatness, that ability is in us.

Romans 8:11, "If the Spirit of Him who raised up Christ Jesus from the dead dwelleth in you, He that raised up Christ Jesus from the dead shall give life also to your mortal bodies through His Spirit that dwelleth in you."

This same Spirit that raised Jesus from the dead does dwell in you. You have asked Him to come in, and He has taken His place in you.

The same ability He had when He raised Jesus from the dead, is in Him now. He can touch that sick and diseased body of yours and make it whole. He can speak through your lips words that will bring salvation to the lost, health and healing to the sick, strength and courage to the defeated. You have the Life-giver in you.

A man is recreated by the Holy Spirit through the Word.

James 1:18, "Of His own will He begat us through the Word." It is the living Word which has given birth to us through the Spirit.

The same Spirit that recreates man has come into you. The same Word that recreates man is in your heart. You are living it now. As you live it, it becomes a living thing, a life-begetting thing in your lips.

I have stood before congregations and seen hundreds of men and women Born Again through the words that passed through my lips by the energy of the Spirit.

I have seen hundreds healed by the words in my lips.

All I said was, "In the Name of Jesus Christ, pain, leave this body. Woman, by His stripes you are healed. Go in peace and praise Him." That simple formula of words from the lips of one in whom He dwells brings healing and salvation.

Col. 1:13-14 illustrates this. "Who delivered us out of the authority of darkness, and translated us into the kingdom of the Son of His love; in whom we have our Redemption, the remission of our sins."

Before the Holy Spirit came to dwell in you, He translated you out of Satan's family and kingdom into the family of the Son of His love.

It is the same Spirit who dwells in you that poured into your spirit Eternal Life and made you a son of God, an heir of God, and a joint heir with Jesus Christ.

John 3:5-8 tells us that it is the Spirit's work to recreate men. It is the Spirit's work to build the love nature of the Father into our very being.

The Holy Spirit has taken us out of the Sense Knowledge realm. You understand what I mean by Sense Knowledge. That is the only knowledge that natural man has, so he denies the knowledge that comes through the Bible.

When the Holy Spirit recreates us, He pours into our spirits the very nature and life of God. We are translated out of Satan's family into God's family.

Phil. 2:13 (20th Century translation), "For it is God who is at work within you, willing and working for His own good pleasure."

God is at work within you, building the love nature of the Father into you, renewing your mind through the Word, healing the sick, and living the Jesus life in you until Romans 8:11 becomes a living fact.

"But if the Spirit of Him that raised up Jesus from the dead dwelleth in you, He that raised up Christ Jesus from the dead shall give life also to your mortal bodies through His Spirit that dwelleth in you."

The life-giving power of the Spirit in you is pouring out health and healing to others around you.

Phil. 4:13 is true in your case. "I can do all things in Him who strengthens me," or "who is my enabling ability."

You have God in you. He is the limitless God. He is the God who made David's aim so accurate that he smote the Phillistine.

He is the God who enabled Elijah to stand in the presence of the angry king and build an altar that He honored by fire from heaven.

He is the same Spirit who wrought so mightily through the early church.

There is a three-fold ministry of the Spirit with each one of us: first, He recreates us; second, He builds the nature and life of God into us; third, He ministers to the world and to the church through us.

Psalms 27:1 is actually fulfilled in us. "Jehovah is my light and my salvation; Whom shall I fear? Jehovah is the strength of my life; Of whom shall I be afraid?"

The Holy Spirit becomes the light, the illumination of your intellect. He illumines your whole spirit nature and your mind.

He is your salvation. He brings you salvation. That means deliverance. He makes Redemption a reality to you, not a theological subject for discussion, but a living reality in your daily life.

He makes you to say, "Of whom shall I be afraid?" The Holy Spirit can make you strong with the strength of God.

I prayed for a woman who had been bedfast for a long time. She immediately got up and came down to the church. That was the Holy Spirit imparting life to that physical body.

1 John 4:4, "Ye are of God, my little children, and have overcome them: because greater is He that is in you than he that is in the world."

It is the love God inside of you, making love greater in you than selfishness and its child, hatred, in the world.

Selfishness and hatred are the blighting curses of the human race.

The indwelling love God is the only cure for selfishness. This is the very genius of Christianity. It is God in us, His ability in us.

He takes the weak, the useless, and the outcast, and makes them the leaders by filling them with Himself. He takes common men and makes them supermen.

He made mere fishermen to become empire builders, and a tent maker to be the voice of God!

God imparts to man His ability. He not only recreates him, gives him His life, making him His own very child; but He makes it possible for man to become a partaker of His own wisdom.

I am confident of this, that it is possible for a child of God to so walk in the wisdom and ability of God that he will actually become a superman.

You will know how to use the Name of Jesus, and all the authority invested in that Name.

You will know how to take advantage of the Holy Spirit's presence in your life.

You will know how to take advantage of your privileges as a member of the Body of Christ, and as a child of God.

You will know your standing in Righteousness with the Father, and you will be able to exercise your rights in His presence.

If one could understand the p r i v i l e g e that Righteousness gives to every child of God, it would revolutionize the church over night.

Chapter The Twenty-second

A NEW CLASS OF MEN

"THERE were giants upon the earth in those days."

How the imagination plays with a statement like that. They were physical giants.

We have mental giants in our day, but the world's greatest giants are spiritual giants . . . giants in the realm of faith. They belong to the new order.

In Way's translation of Phil. 1:17 he tells us, "Those who are animated by love do it because they know that I am the appointed champion of the Glad-tidings."

How my heart thrilled over that. "The appointed champion of the Glad-tidings of Christ."

If we could get together all the statements that the Father made through Paul, John, and James about the New Creation, I think it would stagger you.

He opens the drama with Col. 1:13-14. Let me give you Way's translation of it: "He hath rescued us from the tyranny of darkness, and hath transferred us into the Kingdom of the Son of His love, in whom we have our ransoming, the remission of our sins."

Notice what we are. We have been translated out of the thralldom of Satanic dominion. We have been born of God by the Spirit. We have been born into the Family of God. We have received remission of everything that we ever did in our past lives. We have been made New Creations, created in Christ Jesus.

It is our spirit, our real self, "the hidden man of the heart," that has been recreated. We have become a New Spirit, a New Self, a New Creation.

Our Theologians have never grasped this. They have never understood that we had anything beyond forgiveness of sins. If that is all we have, then the sin nature that required a Substitute has never been removed. It is still dominant in us.

The Word declares, "Wherefore if any man is in Christ, there is a New Creation, the old things have passed away, Behold, they have become new."

Did you notice that strange word, "Behold"? That is an exclamation of surprise and wonder. Have you taken it in? Something has happened in us.

We have become partakers of the Divine Nature, and our past has stopped being. We are New Creation people.

In the first creation, (recorded in the first chapter of Genesis,) it took six days to make the first creation. It took three days and three nights to perfect the New Creation.

I want you to notice carefully that everything in that first creation was the work of God. Everything in this New Creation is of God, man had no part in it . . . only that he accept it.

I wonder if you have ever noticed Way's translation of Col. 1:9-12. It is so striking and literally true that I want to quote it.

"For this reason I too, ever since the day I heard of you, have not ceased to pray for you. I ask God that you may have in full measure that perfect knowledge of His will which is an essential of all true wisdom, of all spiritual intelligence. I ask Him that you may pass through life in a manner worthy of our Lord, so as to please Him entirely. I ask that in every good work you may, as trees of His planting, still be bearing fruit, still growing higher, in the perfect knowledge of God. I ask Him that with all His strength you may be strengthened, even to the measure of the might of His divine majesty, till you attain to all-enduring patience and forbearance, which exults under suffering, I ask that you may ever render thanksgiving to the Father, who has made us fit to have a share in the inheritance of His consecrated ones who walk in light."

The Spirit knew that some of the New Creation folk would doubt the reality of the New Creation, and so through Paul's lips He prays this remarkable prayer, that we New Creation people may be filled with the exact perfect knowledge of His will, and it was to be in all spiritual wisdom and understanding.

You understand, knowledge is gained through study and observation, but wisdom is a thing that only God can give to us; it comes with Eternal Life. It is part of the equipment, or accessories, of the Divine Life.

We would never know how to use the ability that belongs to us, nor enter into our inheritance, or enjoy the riches of His grace, without special wisdom.

So He says these remarkable words, "He has given us the ability to enjoy all that belongs to us in that remarkable redemptive work."

Now with joy I realize that I am delivered out of the authority of Satan as Israel was delivered out of Egypt.

I have been born out of Satan's family into God's family. I am as much a child of the Father as was Jesus during His earth walk.

I have the nature of the Father, I have the love that dominated the life of the Master, and I have the wisdom of God in Christ.

He is now the strength of my life. He has given to me His own ability. I have a legal right to the use of the Name of Jesus, and all authority in Heaven and on earth is in that Name.

I am fully equipped. The living Word is on my lips and in my heart. He is now building Himself into me through the living Word.

A confession like this instantly separates you from the old life of failure and weakness.

When I have been thoroughly instructed that the old things of weakness are passed away, and I can now walk in the reality of the New Creation life; when I am made to know that I am a branch of the Vine, and that the very Vine Life of Jesus is flowing through me, and that I possess certain rights and privileges in Christ, then I will rise to the level of it.

If I have only been taught that my sins are forgiven, and that I have been justified, and that I will only remain justified if I walk carefully, and have never been taught that I have the nature and substance of God in my spirit, and that I am actually a New Self, a New Creation, then sin and Satan will continue to reign over me.

In Phil. 1:11 Paul was unveiling himself to that little group of believers at Philipi. Way's translation is striking. He says that "he has the heart cry of his Messiah."

He says, "this is my prayer, that your love may rise higher and higher to its fullest development in the recognition of the truth and in comprehensive grasp of its application, thus furnishing you with a sure test of what is true excellence, so that you may remain untainted by error, unstumbling amidst obstacles, till the Day of Messiah's Appearing, (it is the next sentence that gripped my heart) bearing the while a full harvest of righteousness attained through Jesus our Messiah."

How few of us have ever really realized what Righteousness has meant to us. The word "Righteousness" means the ability to stand in the Father's presence without the sense of guilt or condemnation . . . to be able to stand in the presence of Satan and his works without the sense of inferiority or fear.

Romans 3:26 (margin of American Rev. Version) shows us that God Himself becomes the Righteousness of the man who has faith in Jesus.

In 1 Cor. 1:30 Jesus is made unto us Righteousness.

In 2 Cor. 5:21, "Him who knew no sin God made to become sin that we might become the righteousness of God in him."

In the 17th and 20th verses he shows us how we have become the righteousness of God in Him. It is by receiving the nature of God. All the attributes of that wonderful nature of love and grace have been imparted to us in the New Birth. Is it any wonder that he says, "Of his fulness have we all received and grace upon grace."

In Col. 2:9, "For in him dwelleth all the fulness of the Godhead bodily."

"In Him are ye made full (or complete)."

This New Man is no ordinary product of modern educational facilities or of modern civilization. He comes out of the womb of God. He is born of God. He is a New Creation created in Christ Jesus.

But that is not all. As soon as he is Born Again, Recreated, and becomes a New Creation, he may become indwelt by the great mighty Holy Spirit who raised Jesus from the dead.

1 Cor. 6:19,20 "Or know ye not that your body is a temple of the Holy Spirit which is in you, which ye have from God? and ye are not your own; for ye were bought with a price: glorify God therefore in your body."

We have a legal right to invite Him to come and take possession of us.

Remember that Jesus said in Luke 11:13, "How much more will your heavenly Father give the Holy Spirit to them that ask Him."

You see, it is His children to whom the promise is made. It is His children who will ask the Holy Spirit to come into their bodies.

We are born of the Holy Spirit. The Holy Spirit has imparted to us the nature and life of the Father, which makes us New Creations, gives us a New Self. Then we are indwelt when we invite Him to come into our bodies, and make His permanent home there.

There is no need to tarry for the Holy Spirit, for He is already here. They tarried on the Day of Pentecost for His coming; He had not yet made His appearance; but He is here now.

You could not be Recreated without Him. You are born of the Holy Spirit, and now you have a right to ask His indwelling. He will come in now and make His home in you.

You had to become a child of God, a New Creation, first. He did that by imparting the nature of the Father to you. Now He wants to make His home in you; can you imagine what it would mean!

Turn to 1 John 4:4 and notice this scripture carefully. "Ye are of God my little children, (you see, you have been born of God, you came out of Him, and are part of Him) and greater is He that is in you than he that is in the world."

Who has come into you? The great, mighty Holy Spirit.

Remember Romans 8:11? "And if the Spirit of Him who raised up Christ Jesus from the dead dwell in you, He who raised up Christ Jesus from the dead is giving life to your mortal body."

You cannot be a failure with Him in you. You may not always take advantage of His presence, you may not always remember that He is there, but He IS THERE, and He is the one whom Jesus promised.

He said, "When he, the Spirit of truth is come, he will guide you into all truth. He shall take the things of mine and reveal them unto you." John 16:13.

I prefer this translation, "When He, the Spirit of reality is come, He will guide you into all reality."

The reality of the New Birth, the reality of your Redemption, the reality of your relationship to the Father, and the reality of the living Word.

What a wonderful thing it would be if the Word would become a living thing on your lips. It will be if you will let it be, and you will let it be because that is joy and victory!

I should not have said, "if you let it be," for that savors of our modern preaching. They tell us what we could do "if we had faith," and "if" we would live right we could have this, and we must give up this to be that. I preached that way for years, until one day I saw what God had made me to be in Christ. I saw what He had given me in Christ.

I will never forget the hour when I sat at my desk and wrote some of the things I am in Christ.

"I am indwelt of God; I have His nature and life." And then I wrote this, "I am what He says I am. He is in me what He says He is. He can do through me what He says He can do."

I trembled as I read it.

Then I saw this glorious fact: I did not need to have faith for what already belonged to me, what had already been given to me, and for the things that the Holy Spirit was ready to guide me into.

I did not need faith for these things because they were already mine.

I did not need faith to use the Name of Jesus, all I needed was courage to use what belonged to me.

The Master said, "In my name ye shall cast out demons and lay hands on the sick, and they shall recover."

Then I remembered Col. 1:12. He had given me ability to enjoy all that belonged to me in Christ.

Let us go back to 1 John 4:4, "Greater is He that is in you than he that is in the world."

Who is in me? Love is in me and God is love. Jesus was love manifested in His earth walk. The Holy Spirit is Love. Greater is love in me than the hatred and bitterness and jealousy that is in the world.

This New Creation man is the Righteousness of God. He has the ability of God. He can dominate the forces of darkness. He reigns as a king in the realm of life, through Jesus Christ.

"Who is he that overcometh the world? He that is born of God."

Take Weymouth's translation of Romans 5:17, "For if through the transgression of one individual, death made use of the one individual to seize the sovereignty, all the more shall those who receive God's overflowing grace and the gift of Righteousness, reign as kings in the realm of life through the one individual, Jesus Christ."

You see, spiritual death is the nature of the devil, and spiritual life is the nature of the Father God.

Jesus came that we might receive Eternal Life, and be taken out of the thrall of Satan and into the family of God.

Jesus said, "The prince of this world cometh to me, but he has nothing in me."

I wonder if you have ever realized that since you are a New Creation and have come into the family of God, that Satan has nothing in you. He has no ground to enter the sacred precinct of the New Creation. If he does enter, it is because you have permitted him to do so.

We have had a limited picture of the New Man with God's life, God's wisdom, God's love and grace, in Christ.

No man can be a success who is not governed by love, the Jesus kind of Love.

Faith, Love and Wisdom are born of the re-created human spirit.

When the human spirit becomes a partaker of the nature of God, you can see the limitlessness of it.

If it were developed, it would make this re-created man a superman.

It links him up with Omnipotence.

Mark 16:17-18 "And these signs shall follow them that believe: in my name shall they cast out demons; they shall speak with new tongues; they shall take up serpents, and if they drink any deadly thing, it shall in no wise hurt them; they shall lay hands on the sick, and they shall recover."

These words filled with faith, born of your spirit, now are spoken with your lips, and the same kind of results follow that Jesus promised.

God-filled words, faith-filled words, but words spoken by common human lips, produce miracles.

Chapter The Twenty-third

SOME CHARACTERISTICS OF THE SUPERMAN

AN was not created for slavery or bondage. To be weak is to be a slave. To be in want is to be in bondage. God's first man was what we would call a superman, a man who lived in the supernatural realm; not necessarily all the time, but whenever supernatural ability was necessary, he could draw on it.

The Old Covenant began with the superman, Abraham. At ninety-nine years of age, Abraham had his youth renewed, and Sarah had her youth renewed at ninety years of age.

In every generation of Israel's history, as far as we know, there were men who at times entered into the supernatural realm. Men who dared to obey the voice of an angel.

In the deliverance of Israel, Moses exercised supernatural gifts: the opening of the Red Sea, the mighty miracles in the desert, and perhaps the greatest miracle was that when Moses died at the age of one hundred and twenty years, his natural forces were not abated. He did not die of disease. He had finished his work and Jehovah took him.

Joshua was a supernatural man at times. His crossing of the Jordan, the fall of the walls of Jericho, the sun standing still, all these were acts of a faith transcending the natural.

Samuel, Elijah, Elisha, Daniel, and the three Hebrew children, all were supermen. They were common men in exterior; they lived as common men until some great demand was made upon them. Then they rose to the lofty height of faith that dominated circumstances and people around them.

Jesus was a superman. From His Baptism, until His Resurrection, He lived above natural laws. He ruled them at His will. He walked upon the sea, He hushed the storms and the winds, He controlled the fish at will. He fed the multitude with five loaves and two little fish. He healed the sick, He raised the dead,

He caused maimed limbs to become whole once more. He was the absolute master of all the laws of nature.

Perhaps the most staggering miracle of His ministry was the raising of Lazarus whose body had begun to decay. For four days that body had been in the tomb, and Jesus, as simply as I would ask you to pass me a book, said, "Lazarus, come forth."

He was the absolute master of death.

The most significant thing about the ministry of Jesus from this angle was what He said about those who were to believe on Him.

Matt. 19:26 "With God all things are possible." Here, the God of all flesh, with whom all things are possible, is brought into contact with humanity in the person of Jesus. This all powerful God is the one with whom we deal.

John 17:2 "Even as thou gavest Him authority over all flesh, that to all whom thou hast given Him, He should give eternal life."

Jesus had authority over all flesh. Jesus and the Father were one in their mighty purposes and ministry.

In Matt. 17:21, when Jesus was speaking to the disciples He said, "And nothing shall be impossible unto you." Jesus was either speaking carelessly, or He was declaring a great truth. We believe He spoke a great truth.

Something was going to happen to them that was going to bring them into the class with God.

"All things are possible with God," and, "Nothing shall be impossible unto you."

Mark 9:23 "All things are possible to him that believeth." That word "believeth" is the same word that we get in Mark 16:17, "And these signs shall accompany them that believe."

It really means "a believing one," one who has accepted Christ as Saviour and Lord, who has been recreated, come into the family of God.

"And these signs shall accompany them that believe: in my name shall they cast out demons; they shall speak with new tongues; they shall take up serpents, and if they drink any deadly thing, it shall in no wise hurt them; they shall lay hands on the sick, and they shall recover."

Jesus promised that in His Name the disciples should be supermen.

There is no escaping this. No matter what the churches teach today, here is the fact:

19th verse, "So then the Lord Jesus, after He had spoken unto them, was received up into heaven, and sat down at the right hand of God. And they went forth and preached everywhere, the Lord working with them, and confirming the Word by the signs that followed."

Some will tell you that the day of miracles has passed. It has passed to the largest part of the Sense Knowledge ruled Church, but it has not passed to anyone who believes the Word and dares to do the things that Jesus has commanded us to do in His Word.

Here we see the utter limitlessness of John 14:12-14. "Greater works than these shall he do; because I go unto the Father. And whatsoever ye shall ask in my name, that will I do, that the Father may be glorified in the Son. If ye shall ask anything in my name, that will I do."

Jesus is not talking about prayer, He is talking about the thing He mentions in Mark 16, "In My Name ye shall cast out demons . . ."

He says, "Whatsoever ye shall ask in my name, that will I do."

Peter standing at the beautiful gate, when the crippled man held out his hands for help, said, "Silver and gold have I none; but what I have, that give I thee, In the Name of Jesus Christ of Nazareth, walk." The man was perfectly healed. It was faith in that name that made him well.

The Name of Jesus in the lips of an uneducated man like Peter made that man whole.

He was greater than disease. He had the authority over disease. He had the ability to change that helpless man whose legs had never sustained his body, so they became normal, so that the man ran, leaping and praising God, into the temple.

He had performed a prodigy. He had made that cripple a new man. That ability has never been withdrawn from the church. It belongs to the church now, in the Name of Jesus.

John 15:16 . "That whatsoever ye shall ask of the Father in my name, he may give it you."

John 16:23-24 "And in that day ye shall ask me nothing. Verily, verily I say unto you, If ye shall ask anything of the Father, He will give it you in My Name."

If language means anything, this means that there is limitless ability in the Name of Jesus, and that limitless ability is given to the man who believes in Jesus Christ.

All it requires is that we act on that Name, that we honor God enough to acknowledge the truthfulness of what Jesus said.

Matt. 18:19-20 "If two of you shall agree on earth as touching anything that they shall ask, it shall be done for them of my Father who is in heaven. For where two or three are gathered together in my name, there am I in the midst of them."

This is another promise of supernatural ability. It is given to two; if one fails and hasn't ability to take the thing alone, he can get someone else to join with him.

"One shall face a thousand, and two shall put ten thousand to flight," is the promise that was given to the Old Covenant people.

In the New Covenant there are limitless privileges given to the individual believer that were utterly unknown to those of the Old Covenant.

What is necessary in order for us to enjoy the abilities of this supernatural life?

I want to call to your attention several things. They are the same abilities that mark and characterize the ordinary child of God today (because he never uses them, does not bring discredit upon his privileges.)

First: We must be free from Satan's dominion. There is no ground for faith as long as one is conscious of slavery. Faith can only grow in the realm of freedom.

The first thing that Jesus had to do to lay the foundation for a supernatural life was to conquer Satan.

Jesus identified Himself with the human race in order that we, by accepting His great substitutionary work, might be identified with His deliverance.

He became a man, that as a man He might conquer Satan. Then He permitted Himself to be nailed to the cross, and God laid our sin nature, our weakness, our bondage, our fear, yes, laid us upon Him.

2 Cor. 5:21 "Him who knew no sin, God made to become sin; that we might become the righteousness of God in Him."

No man can enjoy the righteousness of God who is in bondage. The very thought of righteousness means deliverance. It means that Satan's dominion has been annulled, abolished and destroyed.

In the great Revelation of Jesus that Paul gives us in his Epistles, he shows us that when Christ was nailed to that cross, we were identified with Him. It was for us that He was nailed there.

We were crucified with Him; we died with Him; we were buried with Him; we actually went to the place of suffering with Him. He was our substitute, He was taking our place. It was as though we were there. His suffering was our suffering.

Then, after He had paid the penalty of our transgressions and made provision for our Justification, He was Justified, declared Righteous. When He was Justified and declared Righteous, it was our emancipation.

He was recreated, "made alive in spirit." That was when we were made alive in spirit and became New Creations in the mind of Justice.

Before He was raised from the dead, He met Satan in his own throne room, stripped him of the authority that Adam had given to him in the garden.

The victory that Jesus celebrated over the adversary, when "He put off from Himself the principalities and the powers," was our victory.

If Jesus conquered the devil, you conquered the devil. It was your victory, not His. He had no reason to fight that battle.

When Jesus conquered Satan and stripped him of his authority, He arose from the dead and shouted to the disciples, "All Hail!" Redemption morn had come to the human.

The instant you take Jesus Christ as your Saviour and confess Him as your Lord, everything that Jesus wrought in those days and nights of suffering, and of triumph and victory, belongs to you.

Then this fact stands out clearly: We are absolutely delivered from the dominion of Satan. As far as we are concerned, Satan has been dethroned, his dominion has been broken.

1 Cor. 2:6, .one translation reads, "the dethroned powers of this age."

That is a very remarkable expression. They were the ones who crucified our Lord. He dethroned them.

Let this become absolutely clear, workable knowledge in your mind. You have been delivered from Satan's dominion. Satan has no right to reign over you.

A Second great fact: I must be able to stand in God's presence free from condemnation, without fear, without the sense of guilt or inferiority.

As long as there is a sense of condemnation, there will be no sense of freedom, there will be no place for faith in develop.

The moment a man knows that he has a legal right to stand in the Father's presence, just as freely as Jesus, that moment Satan's dominion over him ends.

Then Col. 1:13-14 becomes a reality. "Who delivered us out of the authority of darkness, and translated us into the kingdom of the Son of His love; in whom we have our redemption, the remission of our sins."

The instant you know that you have become the Righteousness of God in him, that moment Satan's dominion over you ends.

It is this sense of guilt and sin that robs man of his initiative, robs him of his ability to stand uncondemned in God's presence. If one is condemned in God's presence, he stands condemned and belittled in the presence of sickness, disease and poverty. He is whipped by them.

But if he knows that on the ground of the finished work of Christ he can become a New Creation created in Christ Jesus, and the moment he accepts Jesus Christ God gives to him His own nature, and he becomes the Righteousness of God in Christ and receives Eternal Life, then it is not a problem of feeling or sense knowledge, but a problem of the absolute accuracy and truthfulness of the Word of God.

He knows that he is what God says he is . . . the Righteousness of God in Christ. He is not afraid to walk into the Father's presence. He is not afraid of disease and sickness, of poverty and want. He knows that he is a master.

A Third fact: He must become a New Creation created in Christ Jesus.

I have shown you that there is a Redemption and a Righteousness provided. That Redemption and Righteousness become realities when he becomes a New Creation.

2 Cor. 5:17-18 "Wherefore if any man is in Christ, he is a new creation: the old things are passed away; behold, all things are become new. And all these things are of God, who reconciled us to himself through Christ, and gave unto us the ministry of reconciliation."

That New Creation is a Son of God.

1 John 3:2 "Beloved, now are we children of God." That New Creation is an heir of God and a joint heir with Jesus Christ. That New Creation has received Eternal Life.

1 John 5:13 "These things have I written unto you, that ye may know that ye have eternal life, even unto you that believe on the name of the Son of God."

When one receives Eternal Life, the nature of God, he becomes a member of the body of Christ. He utterly becomes one with Christ, so that John 15:1-8 becomes a reality in his mind.

"I am the vine; ye are the branches." That believing one is a member of the body of Christ. He is just as near Christ as the branch is to the vine. He is just as much a part of God as Jesus was a part of God, just as much a part of God as the branch is a part of the vine.

You are tied up with the ability of God. You are tied up with Omnipotence.

God says, "My thoughts are not as your thoughts." God's mind is above ours.

In Paul's revelation, he says, "We have the mind of Christ."

This New Creation is really in the realm of God. The New Creation recognizes only one Lord, Jesus Christ.

The New Creation has a legal right to all the privileges that were wrought in Christ for man. Everything that Jesus did, and all that Jesus is today, belongs to the New Creation, because the New Creation is a part of Christ.

In 1 Cor. 12:12 we are called the Christ. "For as the body is one, and hath many members, and all the members of the body, being many, are one body; so also is Christ."

In 2 Cor. 6:15 the Church is called the Christ. "And what concord hath Christ with Belial?" The unregenerate man is called Belial, the recreated man is called Christ.

"I am the vine; ye are the branches." The branch is a part of the vine.

A Fourth fact: this New Creation must know his legal rights and standing in Christ.

The Bible is made up of two legal documents . . . an Old and a New Covenant. A Covenant is a contract, an agreement.

The first contract was between Abraham and God; the second contract was between Christ, and the body of Christ (the church), and God.

Jesus' death was a legal death. Substitution was a legal act. The demands of Justice had to be met. Jesus met the demands of Justice; the Supreme Court of the Universe accepted the sacrifice of Jesus Christ as having met the demands of Justice against any man who would take Jesus Christ as Saviour and accept His Lordship over his life.

This legally born child of God has a legal right to use the Name of Jesus. He has a legal right to the indwelling presence of the Holy Spirit. He has a legal right to his place in the family of God, and to his share of the inheritance of the saints in light.

He has a legal right to the ability of God.

All that Jesus was and is, legally belongs to the believer. All that Jesus did and is doing now belongs to the child of God legally.

The child of God has a legal right to the Father's protection and care. He has a legal right to food, raiment, and a home. He has a legal right to fellowship and happiness with the brethren. He has a legal right to reign over Satan and demons, to reign over poverty.

Romans 5:17 (Weymouth) "For, if, through the transgression of the one individual, Death made use of the one individual to seize the sovereignty."

That is spiritual death. Satan seized the supremacy over the human race, seized the sovereignty that Adam had in the Garden.

Adam had dominion over all the work of God's hands. Satan took that away from man. Jesus came and restored that dominion to man.

"All the more shall those who receive God's overflowing grace and gift of righteousness reign as kings in life through the one individual, Jesus Christ."

How much grace have we received? Jesus was God's grace. Grace is love in action, blessing the human race. Great grace was upon the disciples . . . great, divine acts in healing the sick, in performing miracles.

We have received the abundance of His ability to help humanity. We have received the gift of Righteousness, the ability to stand in the Father's presence without the sense of inferiority or fear, the ability to stand in the presence of Satan as a master, to stand in the presence of disease and sickness as a deliverer.

We have received that abundance of grace and this gift of Righteousness. What is the result? We reign as kings in the realm of life through Jesus Christ, our Lord.

It has made masters of us. We, who have been slaves, have now become the rulers.

Common people are entering into the throne room and joining forces with King Emmanuel.

We are dealing with the actual things that belong to the Christian, but have been ignored by the Church.

Today, any man who confesses these things is considered to be a fanatic. Jesus died as a fanatic. Paul died as a fanatic. John and Peter, and all of the rest of the apostles died as fanatics.

People said Paul turned the world upside down. This message will turn the world upside down if men will believe it and act upon it.

The Holy Spirit is ours. As soon as you are Born Again your body is the home of God.

1 Cor. 6:19 "Or know ye not that your body is a temple of the Holy Spirit which is in you, which ye have from God? and ye are not your own; for ye were bought with a price; glorify God therefore in your body."

Glorify Him now by laying hands on the sick, by letting your tongue become the pulpit of God through which He will speak His mighty words.

"The Words that I speak, they are spirit and they are life," said Jesus.

The Word becomes spirit and life in the man who has yielded to the Lordship of Jesus, and in whom the Spirit has absolute sway and rule.

This is a marvelous fact of grace.

Phil. 2:13 "For it is God who is at work within you, willing and working His own good pleasure." (Literal translation.)

You have become the throne room of God, so to speak. Your body has become the pulpit out of which this inside God is ruling.

Oh, that the Church might become God-inside minded. They are weakness minded, they are sickness minded, they are inferiority-complex minded, they are trouble and poverty minded, but they are not God minded.

If you become God minded, then the mind of Christ will become yours. God will think through your mind, and speak through your lips. God will heal the sick with your words and the touch of your hands. You will pass out of the realm of the inferior into the realm of the supernatural.

1 John 4:4 "Ye are of God." I am of God. If I am of God, you may expect me to act like God, to speak like God. You may expect me to dominate and rule demons as God did.

"For greater is He that is in you than he that is in the world." Who is in the world opposing God? Satan is, through men and women. It is not the men and women who are opposing God, it is the demon power that has gained the ascendancy over their minds. We are going to dethrone him.

Jesus dethroned him and he knows it, but he is still holding on to these world minded men.

How are we going to dethrone him? The truth is going to set men free. We are going to unveil the Word so simply, so clearly, and the power of God is going to be so mightily upon it that men and women are going to get their deliverance.

Supernatural men will be dressed as common men, but they will have the ability, the strength, and the wisdom of God in them.

A Fifth characteristic of the superman is that they will love men.

They are begotten of love. God is love. They have received God's nature. They are lovers. They are no longer seeking their own. They live and work as Jesus did.

No matter what their daily tasks, no matter what their station in life may be, these men who are the sons of God are going to love as He would love. They are not seeking their own, they count not the things that are theirs to be theirs, they act as trustees of them.

Jesus is unveiled to the heart of man through the lives of these men.

"It is no longer I that live, but Christ liveth in me."

Do you think that the Lover, Jesus, would live in a man and that that man could be selfish and bitter?

The superman is going to be a lover. The most outstanding feature of the superman is love. It is the Jesus kind of Love. It is Agapa set on fire by grace, that is reaching through men's lips and men's acts after lost men.

He is not only the super-lover, but he is the Son of God, and God is not only a love God, but He is also a faith God.

Heb. 11:1 "Now faith is giving substance to things hoped for, a conviction of things not seen."

Faith is giving substance to a thing that has never been real as yet. As long as you "hope" for it, it is not real. You never hope when you have reality. Hope is always in the future. Faith is now. Faith is changing the base metal into the purest gold.

3rd verse, "By faith we understand that the worlds have been framed by the Word of God so that what is seen hath not been made out of things which appear."

The universe was brought into being by the Word of God. That agrees with John 1:1-2. "In the beginning was the Word, and the Word was with God, and the Word was God. The same was in the beginning with God."

Turn back to Genesis 1, and notice all God said was, "let there be," and things came into being. A universe came into being by the Word of God. The vegetable world came into being, the animal world came into being by His Word.

We are the sons of a faith God. Our words are to be faith words. We are to take His words as Peter did when he said to the man at the gate of the temple, "In the Name of Jesus Christ of Nazareth, walk." He was taking the words from the lips of the Master.

You bring health and strength where weakness has held control. You bring success where failure has dominated. You bring plenty where poverty has run riot. The days of poverty and weakness are over. We have the strength of God.

Phil. 4:19 "My God shall supply every need of yours according to His riches in glory in Christ Jesus."

The end of want has arrived because we know how to change the baser metals into the purest in Jesus Christ.

This New Creation must learn the secret and joy and blessing of using the Name of Jesus: as you would use a wrench to tighten a nut on a bolt, as you would use a knife to cut a piece of meat.

You dare to use the Name of Jesus to bring healing and deliverance. You dare to step out of the realm of the Senses into the realm of the Spirit and begin to act as the sons and daughters of God Almighty should act.

Chapter The Twenty-fourth

CAN THERE BE ANY IMPOSSIBILITIES TO US IN CHRIST?

OU remember that Jesus said, "All things are possible to him that believeth." He walked in the spirit realm, and that is our realm today. What a challenge this is to the believer.

The Greek word "believeth" means a "believing one."

There never were any "believing ones" until the family of God came into being on the Day of Pentecost, so every one that comes into the family is called, "a believing one."

Jesus, in that declarative statement, has issued a challenge to us; a challenge for us to live in the realm of the spirit; or, in other words, to live in the realm of miracles.

Now, notice a few facts. We have God's nature . . . Eternal Life. This puts us into God's class of being. We have become by a New Creation the very sons of God.

When He says that we are heirs and joint heirs with Christ, we know that it is no metaphysical statement, but a statement of fact.

Romans 4:13 tells us that "Jesus is the heir of the world."

No one knows the limits of the possibilities of the sons of God. We not only have God's nature in us, but the great, mighty Spirit who raised Jesus from the dead has made His home in us. And "greater is He that is in us, than he that is in the world."

That "he that is in the world" is Satan. The "He that is in us" is God. We have limitless possibilities.

The Church has been governed by Sense Knowledge philosophy. They have a philosophical Redemption, a philosophical New Birth, a philosophical relationship with God as Father. Only a few men have come into the realization of the realities of these mighty spiritual forces.

Let it be understood that spiritual forces are greater than physical. A Spirit created material substance, such as the world with all its minerals, metals and chemicals. This was brought into being by God, and God is a Spirit.

Satan is also a spirit. He is the author of all the confusion, sin, wars, hatreds, jealousies, and every other wicked thing.

God is greater than Satan, and He has imparted to man, in the New Birth, His own nature.

Jesus said a phenomenal thing when He gave the Great Commission as recorded in Mark 16:17, "In My Name, ye shall cast out demons."

He lays down a law, and by this law, the believer is greater than demons, because he can cast them out. If he can cast out demons, then he is master of Satan. If he is master of Satan, then he is master of any of the works of Satan.

Satan is the author of sickness, the author of wars and all the unhappiness and misery in this old world.

If the Word means anything to us, then we are masters of the circumstances and the forces that are governing the world today.

The Church has not recognized it. The Church has been dabbling with unbelief. It has been praying for faith . . . the most absurd thing for which man ever prayed.

"But," you say, "the disciples said, 'O Lord, increase our faith'." Yes, but they were Jews under the First Covenant, with unregenerated spirits. You cannot find any such folly as that in the Pauline Revelation.

He calls his Revelation, the "Word of Faith," and it is the Word of faith. It is the Word that produces faith, that gives birth to faith.

Eph. 1:3 "Blessed be the God and Father of our Lord Jesus Christ, who hath blessed us with every spiritual blessing in the heavenly places in Christ."

When you need a thing, you do not have to ask for faith to accept it, do you?

Well, if you knew the Word of God was absolutely safe and reliable and could be acted upon as the word of a bank or any other large corporation, prayer would be a different thing, wouldn't it?

If you knew that no Word from God was void of power; if you knew that Isaiah 55:11, which reads, "So shall my word be that goeth forth out of my mouth; it shall not return unto me void, but it shall accomplish that which I please, and it shall prosper in the thing whereto I sent it," could be utterly depended upon; that no Word from God is void of fulfillment; that He watches over His Word to make it good; that the Eternal Throne is founded upon His Word; and Jesus is declared to be the surety of the New Covenant; and that Jesus is the surety of every word from Matthew to Revelation; and His throne is back of it, and His integrity is enwrapped in it; if this were real to you, then you would have no faith problem.

The Word of God is a part of God Himself.

In John 14:13-14 Jesus said, "And whatsoever ye shall ask in my name, that will I do that the Father may be glorified in the Son. If ye shall ask anything in my name, that will I do."

You know that the word "ask" here means "demand." It is just as though Jesus said, "Whatsoever you demand in my name, I will make good."

That is not prayer. When Jesus talks about prayer, we have it recorded in John 16:23, "And in that day ye shall not pray to me, but verily, verily, I say unto you, if ye shall ask anything of the Father, He will give it to you in my name." That is prayer.

You are to go to the Father in that Name. Jesus has told us that whatsoever you ask of the Father in that Name, the Father will give you.

The other Scripture has reference to demanding demoniacal forces broken over men's lives, like Paul casting the spirit of divination out of the woman, which is recorded in the sixteenth chapter of Acts; or Peter and John saying to the man at the Beautiful Gate, "In the Name of Jesus Christ of Nazareth, walk."

They performed so many miracles in that Name that the Sanhedrin arrested them and commanded them not to preach or teach in that Name.

That Name was the mightiest force in the entire country at that time, and that Name has lost none of its power or authority.

He has given us, "the believing ones," the Power of Attorney to use it. In that Name, we may cast out demons, heal the sick, break Satan's dominion over men's lives.

We have another mighty weapon called the Sword of the Spirit.

THE LIVING WORD

That Word in our lips saves lost men, brings courage and victory where defeat has reigned as a king, produces faith in the faithless, hope in the hopeless, gives courage and mastery to brokenhearted men.

That Word in our lips has creative energy and power.

It is not a problem of faith; it is a problem of our acting, fearlessly and intelligently, on what God has spoken.

Before Jesus went away, He said to the disciples, "Tarry ye in Jerusalem until ye be clothed with power from on high."

Acts 1:8 "But ye shall receive power, when the Holy Spirit is come upon you."

The Greek word translated "power" there means "ability."

Now note, "I want you to tarry in Jerusalem until you receive ability from on high." That will be God's ability.

You are to have God's ability in you . . . God's ability to speak, to use the Name of Jesus; God's ability to understand the Scriptures; God's ability to do His will; His ability to face the world with fearless confidence; also to suffer any kind of persecution without yielding a particle.

God took uneducated fishermen and gave them His ability, His wisdom.

They had the knowledge of their earth walk with Jesus. They had knowledge of His actual death and Resurrection. They had knowledge of what happened on the Day of Pentecost. Now He becomes their wisdom to use that knowledge; and how they used it!

How they shook the very foundations of the Roman Government and the Jewish nation.

They had God's ability, they had God's life that flowed out of God's nature which was imparted to them. They had ability to walk in love, to walk in the Word.

What mighty men the ability of God made out of common, uneducated fishermen!

Col. 1:13 "Who delivered us out of the authority of darkness, and translated us into the kingdom of the Son of His love; in whom we have our redemption, the remission of our sins."

REALITY OF REDEMPTION

Our Redemption was a reality.

God's Son became Incarnate, went on the Cross, went down into Hell as our substitute. When He had satisfied the claims of Justice against the human race, He was justified because He had wrought the thing for which He was sent. He was made alive in spirit, actually re-created.

God said, "Thou art my Son. This day have I begotten Thee."

That was not His birth through Mary. That was His birth out of Spiritual Death, out of Satanic dominion down in the dark regions of the lost.

There He was justified, was made alive in Spirit. There He put off from Himself the Principalities and Powers, and He conquered the forces of Hell, absolutely defeating them. He left Satan and his cohorts absolutely defeated, stripped them of their authority, and then He arose from the dead.

He said, "I am he that liveth, and was dead; and behold, I am alive for evermore; and I have the keys of death and of Hades."

When He arose from the dead, He was master of Satan and of all Hell.

He had redeemed us out of the hand of the Enemy.

Now you can understand that we are delivered out of the authority of darkness.

Satan is darkness. Jesus is the light of life.

We were not only redeemed out of darkness, but we were translated by the New Birth into the Kingdom of the Son of His love.

It is in this Son of His love that we have our perfect Redemption. In the mind of the Father, you are as perfectly redeemed from the hand of Satan as Jesus was when He arose from the dead.

In Eph. 1:7-23, you catch a glimpse of the utter reality of this Redemption. "In whom we have our redemption through

His blood, the remission of our trespasses, according to the riches of His grace."

This Redemption is "according to the riches of His grace."

The believer is just as really redeemed from the hand of the Enemy as Israel was from the authority and dominion of Egypt when they crossed the Red Sea.

Satan has no dominion over our finances unless we permit it. He has no dominion over our physical bodies unless we permit it.

He has no dominion over our spirits to keep us in bondage and give us the sense of inferiority and unworthiness, because we have been made New Creations in Christ Jesus and have become the Righteousness of God in Christ.

When we know the truth, then the truth sets us free.

Eph. 1:22,23 "And He put all things in subjection under His feet, and gave Him to be head over all things to the church, which is His body, the fullness of Him that filleth all in all."

His feet means the Church. For we are His body, and He is the head of that body. He put all things in subjection under the Church, which is His body. That Church is the fullness of Him that filleth all in all.

No one knows what the Church really means to the heart of the Father. No one knows what it means to Christ. He gave His own life for it! The Father gave His own Son for it!

It was not His purpose that the Church should be a bunch of weaklings over whom the Devil could reign and dominate.

No. The body has the same authority that Jesus had in His earth walk.

The body of Christ, individually, have the same ability, as far as dealing with sickness and disease and the works of the Devil, that Jesus had in His earth walk.

Satan's Dominion Is Broken

It is the new era of freedom for man.

John 8:36 has become a glorious reality. "If therefore the Son shall make you free, ye shall be free indeed."

If the Son shall set you free, you are free in reality, and the Son has set us free!

What are we going to do with our freedom?

We want to be sure of one thing . . . that we have not received the grace of God in vain, that we are taking advantage of our rights and privileges in Christ.

Do you understand Romans 3:24? "Being justified freely by His grace through the Redemption that is in Christ Jesus."

"Justified" means "declared righteous," "made righteous."

"Being therefore made righteous by His grace through this marvelous Redemption that is wrought in Christ Jesus."

It is a limitless thing.

Now I want you to turn with me to 2 Cor. 5:17-21, "Wherefore if any man is in Christ, there is a New Creation: the old things are passed away; behold they are become new. And all these things are of God."

Or, as Way translates it, "And of all this, God is the source. He reconciled me to Himself by the mediation of Messiah. He has assigned to me the office of this reconciliation, the charter whereof is: 'God was present in the Messiah reconciling to Himself the world, cancelling the record of their transgressions.' And the message of this reconciliation He entrusted to me. I am acting therefore as Messiah's ambassador. It is as though God were pleading with you by my mouth. As Messiah's representative I implore you, Be reconciled to God. Jesus knew not sin, yet God made Him to be the world's sin with our sins, that we whose sin He had thus assumed might become by our union with Him the very righteousness of God."

Notice the ring of reality in this whole translation of verses 18-21.

"God was present in the Messiah, reconciling to Himself the world, cancelling or wiping out the record of their transgressions." What a declarative statement!

When you become a New Creation, there is nothing in the books against you. It has all been wiped out.

The message of this reconciliation He has entrusted to you and to me. We are acting therefore as the ambassadors of Heaven.

Now I want you to notice what this New Creation is. It was created in Christ Jesus.

Eph. 2:10 "For we are His workmanship, created in Christ Jesus."

Did you notice that we are His workmanship, just as much as Adam was His workmanship? We are actually born of the Spirit. We are actually partakers of the very nature and substance of God. We have become the very Righteousness of God in Him.

Read Way's translation once more.

"Jesus knew not sin, yet God made Him to be the world's sin for our sins, that we whose sin He had thus assumed might become by our union with Him the very righteousness of God in Christ."

We have become the very Righteousness of God.

The thing that has held us in bondage all of our lives has been Sin Consciousness, the sense of unworthiness. Our ministers have preached sin instead of Righteousness.

Whenever they mention Righteousness, they carry the thought of our "being right" and "doing right" rather than our being made, by the New Creation, the very Righteousness of God, and that there is no longer any Sin Consciousness to disturb us and keep us in bondage to the Adversary.

1 Peter 1:23 "Having been begotten again, not of corruptible seed, but of incorruptible, through the Word of God which liveth and abideth."

WHAT WE ARE IN CHRIST

Now we get this thing clearly.

We have the same Eternal Life that Jesus had, for Jesus declares, "I am the Vine and ye are the branches." We have the Vine Life in us. We have the substance in us that was in Jesus.

Jesus has become our Redemption and our Wisdom. Jesus now becomes the ability of God in us so that we are wiser than the Adversary.

The next great fact is that we have God in us.

John 14:16, 17 "And I will pray the Father, and He shall give you another Comforter, that He may be with you forever, even the Spirit of truth: whom the world cannot receive; for it beholdeth Him not, neither knoweth Him: ye know Him; for He abideth with you, and shall be in you."

John 16:13,14 "Howbeit when He, the Spirit of truth, is come, he shall guide you into all the truth; for He shall not speak from

Himself; but what things soever He shall hear, these shall He speak: and He shall declare unto you the things that are to come. He shall glorify me: for He shall take of mine, and shall declare it unto you."

Notice, the Spirit is to glorify Jesus in us, for He is going to take the things of Jesus and build them into us. He is going to be our teacher. But He is going to be more than the word "teacher" actually means. He is going to be an imparter of the very nature of the Father. He is going to build into us the nature and characteristics of Christ.

The Father is love. He is going to build love into us until all our actions and words will be love-colored and love-filled.

Then He is going to be wisdom to us. The wisdom of the Father is unveiled in the Word. He is going to build wisdom into us so that we will be able to act wisely in every circumstance.

We are going to be like Jesus. We are going to have His ability and wisdom, and we will rest quietly in Him. We will have His confidence in the Father. It will no longer be a problem of faith, it will simply be a problem of recognizing the Father's will. We will know that we have the ability to do it.

How big that will make life! How real it will make it!

The old struggle to get faith and to be good will be a thing of the past.

All this is wrought in the recreated human spirit, the "hidden man of the heart."

We will be able to live and walk with the Master. He is going to open the Word to us until it will become a living reality. It will not be just a book, it will be a living thing, living and active in every phase of our daily life.

1 John 4:4 will become a conscious reality to us.

This Will Be Real

"Ye are of God, my little children, and have overcome them: because greater is He that is in you than he that is in the world."

When we awaken in the morning, we will remember, "I will conquer today, for I have His wisdom. I have His ability. I have the great mighty Spirit who raised Jesus from the dead dwelling in me. He will enable me to use the wisdom that is mine. When

I act on the Word, I will do it with a sureness like the sureness that was in Jesus' earth walk. There was no hesitancy there. He knew.

"So now, today, I will know, because all this day the One who raised Jesus from the dead is going to be a motive force in my life. He is going to keep me quiet in hard places. He is going to give me grace; or, in other words, He will teach me how to enjoy the fullness of grace, the fullness of love, and the fullness of joy that are mine."

Can you imagine any limitations or impossibilities to the believer who enjoys what I have already written?

When you realize that we have the same Holy Spirit that Jesus had, the same mighty Name that the Apostles had, the same Living Word, can you not see the limitlessness of this Divine Life?

"All authority" was given to Jesus in Heaven and on earth, so that when we pray in that Name, it moves Heaven, and it conquers anything on earth.

That Name reaches into Heaven. It is known in Heaven.

A little while ago an epileptic came to our services. He had had this disease for years, and he had one of those awful fits in our service.

I took my rights in the Name of Jesus; I cast that demon out.

The man was completely healed, and it has never come back. He had been unable to work, just a burden to himself. Now he is healthy and vigorous and strong.

That is the power, authority and ability that is wrapped up in the Name of Jesus.

We have a legal right to use the Name and to use the Word.

Our Legal Rights

We have a legal right to the ability that belongs to the body of Christ.

I do not know whether or not you have ever realized what it means to you to have a legal right to use the Word, to take your place as a son in the family of God, to exercise your rights.

It will bring glory to the Father and joy to the heart of Jesus.

Jesus said, "The works that I do are my Father's works. The words that I speak are my Father's words." Then He said, "The words that I speak unto you are spirit and are life."

Now, you use that Word just as Jesus used the Father's words. You may fearlessly cast out demons in that Name. The Word declares, "In My Name ye shall cast out demons."

You can fearlessly lay your hands on the sick and know they will recover just as they did when Jesus touched them, just as they did when the early Church touched them.

Jesus is the Word. "In the beginning was the Word, and the Word was with God, and the Word was God."

That Word is Jesus in our lips. When you use the Word, you are using Jesus. When you speak His Word, you are speaking the very thing that Jesus would speak in your place.

Fearlessly take your place. There is nothing impossible to him that believeth. You have come into the realm of miracles . . . NOW DARE TO LIVE THERE AND ENJOY YOUR RIGHTS!

Inspiring Books by E. W. KENYON

THE BIBLE in the light of Our Redemption
A Basic Bible Course

ADVANCED BIBLE COURSE
Studies in the Deeper Life

THE HIDDEN MAN of the Heart

WHAT HAPPENED
From the Cross to the Throne

NEW CREATIONS REALITIES

IN HIS PRESENCE
The Secret of Prayer

THE TWO KINDS OF LIFE

THE FATHER AND HIS FAMILY
The Story of Man's Redemption

THE WONDERFUL NAME OF JESUS
Our Rights and Privileges in Prayer

JESUS THE HEALER
Has Brought Healing to Thousands

KENYON'S LIVING POEMS

THE NEW KIND OF LOVE

THE TWO KINDS OF FAITH

THE TWO KINDS OF RIGHTEOUSNESS

THE BLOOD COVENANT

THE TWO KINDS OF KNOWLEDGE

SIGN POSTS ON THE ROAD TO SUCCESS

IDENTIFICATION

Order From:
KENYON'S GOSPEL PUBLISHING SOCIETY
P.O. Box 973, Lynnwood, Washington 98036